Death Valley Tailings

Death Valley Tailings

Rarely Told Tales of old Death Valley

by George Koenig

Death Valley '49ers, Inc. - 1986

produced by the
SAGEBRUSH PRESS
POST OFFICE BOX 87
MORONGO VALLEY, CALIF. 92256

for the
Death Valley '49ers, Inc.
Death Valley, Calif. 92328

to
BIRDIE

CONTENTS

Contents

ILLUSTRATIONS

COVER ART BY

INTRODUCTION

Come with me back into time. A time when America was young, restless, boisterous, naïve. A time of dreaming of adventures and riches. A time when even ominously named Death Valley lured the daring and desperate.

Fortunately time also softens the harsh, mellows the deadly. No longer does survival in that saline crucible depend upon the meager water supply one could pack, and carefully hoard lest they be another victim found with fingers torn by clawing for water that wasn't there. Today cold drinks are just minutes away.

Now you can bed down in comfort instead of crawling under mesquite clumps to escape the chill and windblown sand. Where once the weary plodded a few miles a day you can speed at 55 miles an hour in air-conditioned luxury over black-topped roads. Where once lives were lost when a wagon broke down, the AAA or a ranger's jeep are now close at hand. With glove-drawered maps you *know* where you are, the distances and directions to where you are going and back without the helplessness, hopelessness of those early travelers who did not.

The romantic, exciting not-so-Good Old Days are gone. But not beyond recall. Recaptured within these pages are stories that will help you to turn back the clock, to relive the historic past. To be aware that there is more to Death Valley than Scotty's Castle, Furnace Creek Inn and Ubehebe Crater. More, too, than picturesque prospectors such as "Shorty" Harris and "Seldom Seen Slim". Or colorful characters like centenarian "Indian George", witness to the Death Valley Party of 1849-50.

Here and there are tantalizing glimpses of shadowy figures oft lost in the time-dimmed pages of history. And of fragmented stories upon which little light has been cast.

In researching *Beyond This Place There Be Dragons*[1], a definitive retracing of the routes of the '49ers across Central Nevada and Death Valley, I was side-trailed many times. Stories surfaced that had to be set aside lest they detract from the primary project. Yet, sparkling like nuggets of high-grade ore on the tailings of Death Valley's history, they could not be discarded and possibly lost in the ever deepening shadows of the past.

This is a definitely different collection of Death Valley tales. Each, some isolated from the others, some linked, helps to provide a more complete picture of one of the most fascinating areas and eras of the Old West.

The 1849ers were the first known men, women, children, white and black, to blunder into then unknown Death Valley. But where man has gone others inevitably follow, despite the deprivations and obstacles. Who were they? When? Why?

From a scattering of accounts, early adventurers Dr. E. Darwin French and Dr. S. G. George are somewhat familiar. But not mysterious Dr. Willing and self-proclaimed "Mountain Man" James Hobbs.

While Lt. Wheeler's topographical expeditions are documented, the boots 'n saddles scouting of Lt. Bendire and Lt. Birnie are buried deeply in the archives.

Men still seek the legendary "Lost Breyfogle Gold" but very few have delved into the accounts of Buel and Todd who met Breyfogle in Death Valley, and whose rare map is one of the earliest of the area. Also unheralded and unsung, is Nevada's Governor Blasdel who, in 1866, purportedly found the bodies of nine '49ers huddled in a pile.

Lest any be prone to point out the omissions of other tales, tall and true, there is an admission that this is not a complete history of

---

[1] Arthur H. Clark Co., Glendale, Calif., 1984.

Death Valley. Rather those of the fascinating lesser known chapters in the lore of what is legendarily known as "Tomesha"—the land of ground afire.

Chapter One

IN THE BEGINNING

Just as all buildings must have a foundation, that of historic Death Valley starts with some lost gold rush emigrants who stubbornly, heroically forged their way across the wastelands of central Nevada into "the valley of death".

Risking repetition, there is a reminder that in the summer of 1849 segments of separated wagon trains had gathered in Salt Lake City, the only settlement of note along the overland trail. Bound for the rainbow's end in the goldfields of California, some had been late in starting westward, others had fallen behind. They milled about amid endless debate. Should they layover or go on? The two year old Mormon colony in the new State of Deseret was hard put to take care of its own let alone a horde of strangers. Supplies were short. Work scarce, especially for transients waiting out several months before continuing west in the Spring.

There were still a thousand miles of trail ahead. Hard, slow travel through a barren little known land. A trail already littered with abandoned wagons, precious belongings and unmarked graves. It was said that one could smell the way by the stench from ox, mule and horse carcasses. There was also a tang to the air that hinted of an early Fall. A reminder of the ill-fated Donner Party that had been trapped by early Sierra Nevada snows in the winter of 1846-47, with 40 or so out of 90 perishing, some surviving by cannibalism.

Then word was heard of a little known southward route, used by pack trains arching a way around the Colorado River canyonlands to link Santa Fé and Southern California. A guide was hired for $10 a wagon. Some 100 wagons, swelled by groups of horse and mule packers, moved out. Mounted men, unencumbered by wagons or families, surged ahead. Stragglers caught up or trailed in the rear. Early attempts to rotate the lead among the wagons, or at least space them out, failed with increasingly meager water sources exhausted by the first arrivals. As far as the eye could see there were billowing clouds of dust as some forged ahead or lagged behind in a constant churning of 300 or so men, women and children and some 500 oxen, horses and mules.

The route was rough and uncertain. It had been almost two years since Jefferson Hunt, the guide, had been over the trail. It was a harsh, parched land where hoped for springs and small streams periodically dry up and disappear. Wind blown sand covered lightly traveled trails. Landmarks, with the passage of time, looked much like countless counterparts. So it was, as they neared present day Cedar City, Utah, word of a shortcut spread like wildfire.

Brought into camp by a group of packers captained by an O. K. Smith, along with a map showing ". . . wood, water and grass at intervals of 12 to 15 miles", it was the answer to many a prayer. It could not only spare them hundreds of miles of torturous trail, but get them to California ". . . before the gold was all gone." Only seven wagons resisted the siren song. The others turned off onto the enticing shortcut.

For a few days all went well until, as '49er William Lewis Manly wrote, "Immediately in front of us was a canyon, impassable for wagons and down into this the trail descended. Men could go, horses and mules perhaps, but wagons could no longer follow the trail." Here, at what they named "Mt. Misery", disappointment, disillusionment and desperation set in. Most turned back to rejoin Hunt and the seven wagons that had kept to the main trail. The shortcutters with only horses and mules descended the steep slopes and wended their way along a deep arroyo towards present day Las Vegas. But 27 wagons managed to work their way westward and into history as the "Death Valley Party of 1849."

Ironically, Death Valley with which they were to be so identified was not to be the great obstacle in itself. It was to be the
climax of a month and a half struggle across sun-scorched wastelands, lost amid seemingly endless bleak mountains, great sandy
valleys and alkalined dry lake beds. When they did reach Death
Valley and looked across that great saline sink they saw not the
verdant California that had been their goal for so long. Instead,
they gazed helplessly, hopelessly at ridge after ridge still barring
their way. Death Valley was, in short, the proverbial straw to
break the camel's back.

Their trek from Mt. Misery from early November to their
eventual arrival in Los Angeles in March, 1850, has been well
told in such books as Manly's classic *Death Valley in '49*[2]. It is in
supplementing them that these stories tell of other lesser known
tales of those who also left their faint footprints in the sands of
Death Valley.

---

[2] The Pacific Tree and Vine Co., San Jose, Calif., 1894, and reprint editions. A list
of recommended Death Valley readings is included as an appendix on page 121.

Chapter Two

13 SKELETONS IN THE SAND

With all of the light that has been cast on the dramatic roles of the Jayhawkers, Manly and Rogers, the Briers and Wades, and the Bennett-Arcan families who survived a month of desperate waiting at the "Long Camp" in Death Valley, some secrets still remain hidden in the deepening shadows.

Such as William Lewis Manly telling of "Thirteen of our party lie unburied in the sands of the terrible dry valley." And that:

> . . . four of the train perished beside the trail, and it will be remembered that one party of eleven started out on foot . . . long afterwards nine skeletons were found at the remains of a camp and the other two were later seen in the gold fields. When spoken to about this party they burst into tears and could not talk of it. So it is known that at least thirteen men perished in the country which has well been named Death Valley.

Thirteen?

The first fatality, substantiated by Manly and Jacob Stover, was that of an unnamed Kentuckian, ". . . buried in as good a style as circumstances allowed" back at Mt. Misery, straddling the Nevada-Utah border. The next, and only known fatality in Death Valley, was that of elderly and ailing "Captain" Culverwell. Later, a Mr. Fisch and Mr. Isham perished in the range west of Death Valley, while nearing Providence Springs. And a William Robinson died, with hope in sight, near the Palmdale-Lancaster area. Since the Kentuckian died before they left Mt. Misery, the other four were those who perished along the way. Which leaves nine to be accounted for.

For this we must turn back to Mt. Misery where they were stopped by "a sheer precipice of a thousand feet or more." Groups of "horse and mule packers," unencumbered by wagons and families, worked their way southerly via Meadow Valley Wash.[3] A loose alliance prevailed until they reached what they named Dead Horse Spring. The going was hard. Food and water gave out. Dissension set in. Some persevered toward the Old Spanish Trail. Some, including O. K. Smith, who many blamed for the ill-fated shortcut, belatedly sought to return to the main trail to rejoin the wagons that remained with the guide, Jefferson Hunt.

Of Dead Horse Spring, Jacob Stover was to write:[4]

> In the morning we killed our first horse to eat, an old gray, one of mine. After breakfast nine concluded to shoulder their guns and take it afoot over the mountains.
>
> I studied the matter over. I came to the conclusion that there were two men in the nine that I would not like to travel with but would be glad to get rid of them both. They were from Iowa City—John Adams [and] Willie Webster. They cut about ten pounds apiece from the old gray horse. I took their names and where they lived . . . five of them lived in Illinois and Missouri; Webster and Adams from Iowa City, Savage from Illinois, Pinney from Ohio. . . .

He later tells of meeting Savage and Pinney in Nevada City where "they gave me the history of those travels after leaving us."

> We went over the mountains and traveled through a rough country, nothing to shoot, not a living thing to be seen, until their horse meat was all gone and we came one night into a camp on a big desert.
>
> The boys said we would have to draw cuts in the morning as to who should be killed to be eaten. As we did not want to be killed to be eaten or eat anybody, when we thought they were asleep we got up and traveled until day, then we took our knives and dug holes in the sand and covered up all but our heads until night when we could come out and travel all night again. . . . We kept

---

[3] Basically the route of the Union Pacific Railroad in later years.
[4] *Trails Divided*, Theo. Ressler, Williamsburg, Iowa, 1964.

westward more than we did before we left those seven men. We had almost given out when we thought we saw water and smoke. That cheered us up and gave us encouragement until we made the lake. It was Owens Lake.

George Cannon, another packer, substantially corroborates Stover except for tallying the nine as eleven.[5]

Eleven resolved to form a company of their own. Their destination was California and in that direction they were determined to travel at all hazards . . . and started westward on foot. Nine went in one direction and two in another. The nine never reached the settlements . . . the two succeeded in crossing the Sierra Nevada mountains and reached California. I met one of these men in the Mariposa mines and from his own lips learned the story of their dreadful sufferings.

Confirming Cannon, another packer, William Lorton, names the eleven as:[6]

Charles McDermot, Kentucky	Mr. Baker, Utica, NY
Mr. Savage, Illinois	Mr. Samore
Jno. Adams	Mr. Allen
G. Wiley Webster	Mr. Moore
J. Ware	Mr. Pinney
T. Ware	

But there are frustrating gaps over the trail from Dead Horse Spring to Owens Lake, and conflicting versions of where Savage and Pinney parted from their companions.

In his *Out West* Magazine article (March 1903), Brier Jr. says:

At the Amargosa they separated, Savage and Pinney steering for the White Mountains and the other nine crossing the Funeral Mountains, entering Death Valley . . .

An earlier item in the *Inyo Independent* (July 26, 1884) clarifies this wasn't something he heard, but witnessed; and that the

---

[5] *A Trip to California*, George Cannon (privately printed, no date).
[6] *Over the Salt Lake Trail in the Fall of '49*, John B. Goodman III and Gordon Holmquist, Zamorano Club Keepsake.

Savage-Pinney Party had caught up by the time the Briers left their wagons just east of the Amargosa:

> After we decided to leave our wagons a company of 11 men, led by Savage and Pinney, pushed ahead . . . near the Amargosa, Savage and Pinney, differing with the rest as to route, remained in camp while their nine companions pushed over into Death Valley. The former were found in a dying condition by Indians, were taken to Owens Lake and recruited; the latter all died in one night and one bed, not far from the center of Death Valley.

One may well wonder about the difference of "route" being the reason for Savage and Pinney parting from the others, compared to the reported threat of cannibalism. And was the incident near the Amargosa, or at McLean Spring in Death Valley where the Jayhawkers, whom the Briers now joined, burned their wagons? Supporting this, Manly was also to note that the party of eleven started out on foot as the wagons were abandoned by the Jayhawkers. And Jayhawker L. Dow Stephens, after telling of the Briers joining them at McLean, continues with:[7]

> Another party of eleven passed us who thought they could make it by packing on their backs enough to last them . . . and out of the eleven there were but two to finish . . .

Another Jayhawker, Charles Mecum, in a January 1872 letter to his fellow travelers, confirms that it was between McLean Spring, "where we burned our wagons and packed our cattle," and "Silver Mountain" where they found the ore that gave birth to the legendary Lost Gunsight Lode. Dramatically he adds that it was here that:

> . . . one other hombre and myself will both remember a long time. Of those boys that left us at Silver Mountain we are disposed to draw the veil, their sufferings were too sickening to dwell upon. I saw Savage afterwards at the mines and his eyes would fill with tears at the mention of that sad time . . .

---

[7] *Life Sketches of a Jayhawker*, L. Dow Stephens, 1916.

To that, Jayhawker Tom Shannon adds an ominous note:

> . . . one man in desperation spoke of casting lots to see which should die for his fellows. He was dealt with severely and never again was such matters broached by any member of the party.

While Shannon does not name the man or his companions, he is repeating Stover's reason for the Savage-Pinney Party breakup, to which he could only witness while in Death Valley.

However circumstantial the evidence, the various accounts give testimonial weight to the Savage-Pinney parting being in Death Valley. Heading westward from Dead Horse Spring they could have caught up with the Briers at the Amargosa and subsequently McLean Spring. The two may well have parted earlier, caught up momentarily before the final fateful parting.

From all who talked to them later, there is no doubt that Savage and Pinney reached the gold "diggings." But what of the other nine?

According to Brier Jr. the nine "all died in one night and one bed not far from the center of Death Valley." Later, in his *Grizzly Bear* article (June 1911) he adds a dramatically embellished postscript:

> Ten years after, Governor Blasdel of Nevada discovered their skeleton remains, side by side, in the undisturbed composure of the last and painless sleep; for in that land of silence Nature, warring upon all forms of life, has imposing regard for the repose of the dead.

Stephens also wrote that ". . . out of the 11 there was but two to finish the trip, the others having died in a pile." And adds an intriguing sequel. That in 1864, while traveling in the Owens Valley, he met a man who had just returned from the Slate Range and told him that some of his party in prospecting had come across the remains of nine men all together behind a little barricade of brush. And that, "I made him promise that he would see the remains properly buried upon his return."

Indefatigable '49er researcher John Ellenbecker, conscientious as he was, probably kept alive the legend of the lost nine from his contacts with the Briers:

> Ten years later Governor Blasdel of Nevada and his searching party found their skeletons just where they composed themselves for that last sleep.

And the rumor was kept alive by Charles Lummis, in his *Mesa, Cañon and Pueblo* in 1925 with:

> Nine young men, stronger than the average of the wasted band, reached this terrible trough ahead of the others and perished with thirst. Years later their bones were found huddled there in a little volcanic bowl . . . by Gov. Blasdel and his surveyors and he gave the name "Death Valley" from this circumstance. Four others of this party also died in this valley.

Much in the same manner did John Spears, in his 1892 *Illustrated Sketches of Death Valley* tell of ". . . several skeletons of men were found by Dr. S. G. George while prospecting in 1860." And in State Mineralogist Hanks' Report of 1883 he tells of "Dr. George . . . found bones of white men within 300 yards of a spring. . . ." Spears appears to be quoting Hanks. But where Hanks got his information is questionable. Nothing has been found of such an incident in Dr. George's material.[8]

Assuredly Governor Blasdel found no skeletons. At least not according to his official reports, published as *Appendix E, Journal of Explorations in Southern Nevada in the Spring of 1866.* Nor is it mentioned in the series of sixteen articles in the Virginia City *Territorial Enterprise*, from March to May 22, 1866, comprising descriptively detailed letters from the various campsites by Correspondent R. Stretch. And newspapermen, especially in those days, were not wont to overlook such sensational tidbits for their readers.

Fiction can become fact through unquestioned repetition. Yet where there is smoke there is oft sparks of fire. It's possible that "of eleven men . . . nine were never seen again." But they may

---

[8] Also see page 36.

have simply melted into the milling mainstreams of miners in the goldfields. Or, as many others, disappeared by returning "Back East." Still, however fancifully, their skeletons may well have been covered by the sands of a vast and empty land.

Typical of Death Valley tales there is a tantalizing footnote to the fate of one. Inyo County historian-writer-publisher P. A. Chalfant, a usually Very Reliable Authority, was to write:

> . . . in the Fall of 1850 the writer, while prospecting around Rough & Ready, Nevada County, paid a visit to his former towns-man and fellow emigrant of '49, Dr. McCormick, who related that a party of young men, among whom were Dr. McCormick, Willie Webster and one or two others of our personal acquaintance, re-turned to Death Valley . . . and related the story of that trip and of the silver mountain . . . and showed us a full handful of this silver. . . .

That the party found the Lost Gunsight silver is dubious. The pre-Fall of *1850* dating doubtful. Even more puzzling is the in-clusion of *Webster* who reportedly perished with the nine.

Still there is a tale, and just that, of Indians watching the '49ers struggling across Death Valley. And one told of going to one of the campsites after the '49ers left and finding the body of a man with a broken leg—shot through the forehead!

It has been theorized that perhaps since the man could no longer walk, couldn't be carried, the act was one of mercy. Or that the victim, traveling alone, with no help at hand, shot himself in despair.

But could it be that this was part of the tale that Manly said, ". . . the worst of it has never been told . . . ?" Could it have been the result of violent life-or-death arguments that may have raged over the proposal to draw lots? Could it be that as some sought to flee one fell in the rocky terrain and broke his leg? Was he the man who was "dealt with severely?"

Is this part of the story behind the story of why it was named *Death* Valley?

☆　☆　☆　☆　☆

Chapter Three

GOLD & SILVER
IN THEM THAR MOUNTAINS

It was early Spring of 1850 when the Death Valley '49ers straggled into the small Pueblo de Los Angeles. But it didn't take long for word to be heard of the "Silver Mountain" they had found, and a cache of gold coins left behind as too heavy to carry.

The time was ripe for glittering temptations. A time when gold fever and silvered dreams were starting to quicken America's pulse. Scatterings of gold and silver had been reported as early as 1579 by Sir Francis Drake. Placerita Canyon, just north of the San Fernando Valley, was the scene of a gold strike in 1842. Then, in 1848, "The Mother Lode" was tapped at Coloma.

Nor was Death Valley immune. Purportedly some of the '49ers who remained with the Hunt train found gold prospects near the Amargosa, giving rise to the rumor of early Mormon mining near Furnace Creek. And Manly was to later repeat a story told to him by John Goller, one of the '49ers traveling with a companion and known as "the two Dutchmen":

> . . . after the wagons were left behind these two men kept together as company for each other . . . while out hunting water one called out, "See what I have found!" The other asked if it was water and the answer was, "No, it is gold." Quickly came the answer, "I want no gold now. I want water and bread that gold will not buy in this dry place . . ."

So, too, with Asahel Bennett, reported as searching for water and finding "plenty of gold."

Little wonder that the tales told about gold and silver discoveries by the '49ers found willing ears.

Ironically, some of the '49ers who had escaped their valley of death were among the first tempted to return. Their mountain of silver, from which a gunsight had been made from a piece of the ore, was to trigger searchings for the Lost Gunsight Lode that have yet to cease.

J. L. West

Manly heard about the Gunsight silver early in 1850, while working for the Reverends Brier and Granger at their "hotel" in Los Angeles:

> The discovery was soon publicly known and on the strength of the report a party was made up [to] locate this wonderful silver mine [which] they believed must be the richest mine on earth. Their guide was one of our party who had just come through, J. L. West, who claimed to know where the piece of silver was picked up. . . .

They found no silver. Frustrated, they threatened to hang West who admitted he had never seen the exact spot where the silver was found.

Turner - Toun

Sometime that same year, ". . . a party of 14, including Turner and Toun" (Towne, Townsend) stopped overnight near Fort Tejon on their way to the Lost Gunsight, at the ranch of Dr. French who Manly and Rogers had met on their rescue trek.

"Toun" had been with the '49er "Georgians" contingent. So, too, was Turner, one of two brothers, who declared:

> I was the one who found it (the silver). I have handled it and know it is native silver for I cut it with a knife and Martin brought some of it away and had a gunsight made of it at the Mariposa mines.

Alas there is no evidence that this group of silver seekers actually reached Death Valley. Only word that they suffered hardships, split into two groups and eventually returned to Fort Tejon.

McCormick - Webster ✔

P. A. Chalfant, publisher of the *Inyo Independent*, authoritative writer on the Death Valley region, and himself a '49er, although via the northern route, tells of visiting an old trail-mate, Dr. McCormick in the Northern California mining camp of Rough & Ready. And was told that McCormick, Willie Webster and some others had returned to Death Valley, found the mountain of silver and showed Chalfant some of the ore.[9]

All things are possible, however prohibitive the odds. But if the McCormick-Webster party had found the Gunsight silver, one wonders why they didn't capitalize on their success. Also suspect is Chalfant being told of it in the *Fall of 1850*, dating the venture as late Spring or Summer, all too few months after the '49ers escaped Death Valley. Even more suspicious is that Webster had reportedly been one of the nine who perished there!

The tangled thread of Dr. William McCormick is interwoven early in Death Valley history. In May 1849 he left Iowa City with the Sacramento Mining Company. Also listed among its members were John, Jacob and Abe Earhart, who wound up at the Death Valley "Long Camp"; and Jacob Stover, one of the "horse and mule packers" who broke away at Mt. Misery along with the Savage-Pinney party.

At Salt Lake City, the Sacramento Mining Company divided; some taking the northern or Humboldt route, the others rejoining Hunt's wagon train over the proposed southern route, including McCormick as "Adjutant" and Rev. Granger who became Brier's partner in Los Angeles.

After a December arrival in Los Angeles, McCormick prospected in the Tulare County area three months later, then moved on to Grass Valley. That he mined unsuccessfully here and resumed his medical practice rather belies finding the rich Gunsight silver that summer. Yet—Rough & Ready is only a few miles from

---

[9]See related information on page 24.

Grass Valley, which fits Chalfant's story whatever the doubt of date, Gunsight discovery and Willie Webster.

Dr. French — 1850 ✔

A more substantiated venture of 1850 is the first of two expeditions by Dr. Erasmus Darwin French who decided to "see the elephant" for himself.

With information from the returning Turner-Toun party, Dr. French and unnamed others set out for the Panamints in September. Proceeding via what became the Coso-Darwin mining area, they crossed into Panamint Valley via Darwin Canyon, named by or for the doctor.

Although they combed the area to which they had been directed they did not find the silver lode. Ironically their route did take them across the silver-rich Coso and Darwin discoveries of a decade or so later. Interestingly, too, mindful of their '49er guidance, it had led them close to the '49ers' life-saving "Providence Springs", indicating the Death Valleyite trail as more northerly than commonly accepted.

☆　☆　☆

The Lost Gunsight was to lure others. Who and how many may never be fully known. Some of it due to the secrecy that surrounds such searchings. Some because such men were not often given to writing, or could not. But stories surface from time to time, fragmented and questionable, of history shadowed men whose obliterated footsteps and unmarked graves cannot be cursorily dismissed.

Such as that of an item in the old *San Francisco Call-Bulletin* that makes a hit and run reference to an unidentified "Hill's Party":

> In the winter of 1859, Hill's party came into Owens Valley. They left part of their party at Lone Pine to prospect while the others crossed over the Inyo Mountains and discovered the Potosi district.

Whether this was a reference to the Potosi Mines southwest

of Las Vegas, worked by Mormons in 1856, is uncertain. But the route to there, from Lone Pine and the Inyos, could have taken them into Death Valley. *Quien sabe?*

Assuredly later miners and adventurers were frequently guided by word or signs of those who had been before. And, in turn, left little evidence of their own. Including the famed "Pathfinder", Colonel John Charles Frémont.

Frémont's Fifth

Frémont was to skirt Death Valley on his relatively little known Fifth Expedition in 1854. Leaving the Mormon settlements of Parowan and Cedar City in early February, Frémont decided to explore an almost due west route ". . . between the 37th and 38th parallels, it recommending itself to me as being more direct toward San Francisco and preferable on that account for a road."

Fatefully traveling a route similar to the '49ers, many of whom had placed faith in Frémont's explorations, he writes:

> . . . we found the country a high table land, bristling with mountains . . . considerable ranges with numerous open and low passes. . . . The valleys are dry and naked, without water or wood; but the mountains are generally covered with grass and well wooded with pines; springs are very rare and occasional small streams are at great distances. Not a human being was encountered between the Santa Clara road near the Mormon settlements and the Sierra Nevada, a distance of more than 300 miles.

Reaching the area of what was to be Goldfield, Nevada, Frémont proceeded across Lida Valley and Eureka Valley, then swung south to the site of Darwin. Although his route now becomes a bit blurred, he apparently scouted two routes. One, invitingly open, via Darwin Wash south to Etcharren Valley and Carricart Dry Lake; the other via adjoining Cole's Flat.[10] From either or both the descent would be along ancient Indian trails of Black

---

[10] Now within the vast China Lake Naval Weapons Center.

or Big Petroglyph canyons into Indian Wells Valley, reaching the Sierra Nevada "about the 15th of March."

As close as he came, Frémont did not enter Death Valley. However, his route across Nevada and southerly from the Darwin-Coso area remarkably approximates that of the 1849ers. That he does not comment on sighting any signs of the '49er trail or campsites is not startling. In that vast desolate land five years of drifting sands may well have hidden them. Or been easily missed in passing even a short distance away.

In his reference to seeking a preferable "road", Frémont is indicating the growing interest in a much debated transcontinental rail route. As did Lt. Williamson's 1853-54 "Reports of Explorations and Surveys to Ascertain the Most Practicable and Economical Route for a Railroad from the Mississippi River to the Pacific Ocean."

Even '49er Rev. Brier was to pontificate before a Pacific Railroad meeting in San Francisco, August 24, 1853, and reported in the *San Francisco Daily Herald* the next day:

> Mr. Bryar [Brier] . . . who had explored the country between the Sierra Nevada mountains and Salt Lake . . . entertained the audience with a narrative of his travels over one of the proposed routes for the railroad . . .
>
> He traced the route from Walker's Pass to Salt Lake, across the desert, and found it entirely practicable. On some parts over which he passed he found beautiful valleys . . . the only obstacle in the way of the road was Owens Mountains, between which and the main chain was a little valley from five to ten miles wide . . . (a route) that can be easily crossed by the railroad . . . the rail cars could run everyday throughout the year . . . [and] expressed a decided preference for this route over all others.

One can but muse than in just three years he seems to have forgotten the difficulties of the '49ers in crossing Central Nevada and the Death Valley region. And that any evaluation as a potential rail route had to consider the lack of a railroad's operating needs for water, wood and coal. Yet he was not as mad as it might seem. Serious thinking did develop over a possible route that inspired the naming of Railroad Valley, canting southwest from Ely toward Tonopah. And just west of that point the Carson & Colorado Railroad was to wend its way over Montgomery Pass into Owens Valley.

Washington Survey

Before closing out the '50s one would be remiss not to touch upon another venture—Colonel Henry Washington's "San Bernardino Meridian Survey" of 1854.

Although specific dates are not known it may be that as Frémont was working his way around the north and west perimeters of Death Valley, a General Land Office survey team was approaching it from the south and the Amargosa usually dry river.

There are those that view its mappings with disdain, primarily for its too conveniently and imaginatively drawn townships and sections in that empty, rugged terrain. Whether or not this was done later at a desk to pad their activities is debatable. Yet the maps do display an authoritative accuracy. Such as the showing of an "old road" in close parallel to the present route through Furnace Creek Wash, basically that taken by the '49ers. Extending from just south of Fairbanks Ranch above Ash Meadows, it is shown crossing the Funeral Mountains just north of the wash, via a pass just east of Pyramid Peak. The same pass that Buel and Todd were to use in 1864-65, as was Lt. Wheeler in the '70s.

That it was noted as an "old road", old even by 1854, strongly indicates it was that of the '49ers. Certainly wheel ruts of their heavy wagons and the passage of some 100 people with oxen would be visible for many years. And there were no known vehicles or large parties in the interim.

That the survey team was not guilty of remote creativity is clued by the mapping of Hadley Springs, after one of the survey members, now known as Travertine Springs. And that the survey team followed the old road to its ending near McLean Spring, where the Jayhawkers abandoned their wagons.

CHAPTER FOUR

THE DICKENSONIAN DECADE

IT WAS, AS Charles Dickens wrote, an ocean away, in 1859—
"... the best of times ... the worst of times ... the age of wisdom
... the age of foolishness."

The Civil War was being fanned into flames in the East. But
in the Far West campfires of fame and fortune seekers flickered in
lonely, desolate regions.

The '60s seemed a psychological outcropping of the fabulous
Comstock Lode discoveries some 300 miles to the north, giving
rise to the belief in a bonanza silver belt extending southward to
the mines of Mexico. Prospectors spread out to found Austin and
the Reese River camps, Silver Peak and Candelaria, Belmont and
Manhattan, Pioche and Treasure City, Aurora and Bodie, and a
host of other tent-towns most of which have long since withered
away.

Mining fever as well as medicine seemed to be in the blood of
two more doctors like Dr. McCormick who, a decade earlier,
sought the Lost Gunsight Lode.

Dr. French — 1860 ✔

In March of 1860, Dr. French, convinced that "If at first you
don't succeed, try again", decided to give the elusive Gunsight
another shot, after licking his wounds for ten years. This time he
guided "The Butte Mining & Exploring Company" of fifteen, including:

Dr. E. Darwin French	Robert Bailey
Dr. W. C. Waldron	Jacob Nash
Minard H. Farley	J. M. (F. L.?) Weston

J. H. (Robert?) Lillard   James Hitchens
W. R. Finch   W. H. Lilley
William McIntyre   "and some others"[11]

They "embarked on a general prospecting tour east of the Sierra Nevada, our paramount object being the rediscovery of a mine of native silver said to have been found within a radius of one hundred miles from Owens Lake in 1849 by a company of lost emigrants."[12]

From Visalia they crossed Walker Pass on April 11. After camping at Little Lake they retraced Dr. French's 1850 route over the Coso-Argus ranges, entering Panamint Valley near Darwin Wash. Unfortunately they were more successful in establishing place names than in locating rich ore.

The following year, Farley, with the group, was to publish his "Newly Discovered Tramontane Silver Mines" map, the first to map-name Death Valley. And Lillard was to be credited with the naming of Telescope Peak.[13] State Mineralogist Hanks, in his June 1, 1883 Report, also credits them with the naming of Furnace Creek:

> . . . so named by the discovery by the party (Dr. French's) of ruined lead furnaces in which the Mormons had extracted lead from Galena to make bullets to be used against the United States troops in 1857.

—a somewhat dubious premise, especially since so much of Hanks' information was from stories told to him.

Too, in proceeding into Death Valley via present day highway #190, they are credited with naming "Townes Pass" after the

---

[11] Joseph E. Doctor, in his authoritative *Dr. E. Darwin French's Exploration of Death Valley*, also names D. M. Harwood, Henry Siddons, Montgomery Smith, Sam Lashley, Charles Uhl and a man named Walweber. That this totals 17 could indicate some dropouts along the way.

[12] Letter from Lillard in the *Oroville Weekly Butte Record*, July 7, 1860.

[13] This has also been credited to "W. T. Henderson of the Boundary Survey Party of 1861." However, Henderson was not a member of that party, nor is it noted in the rather complete accounts appearing in the *Sacramento Union* articles of 1861. However he is listed with the Dr. George expedition of 1860 that followed the French group into the Death Valley area.

leader of the "Mississippi Boys" who had helped trigger Dr. French's 1850 trek.

Descending into Death Valley they camped at a brackish spring where they found relics of the Jayhawker wagons at McLean Spring, "about 25 miles a little west of north from Furnace Creek", and then at Travertine Springs. Whether they continued further south, or eastward to the Amargosa, is conjectural. So, too, with any scoutings westward across the valley. Had they done so they might have coincidentally encountered the Alvord-Bennett-Manly quests for the Gunsight and equally lost "Alvord Gold."

Returning to Little Lake they left two more marks in history. The first literally. They veered into Jayhawker Canyon, probably guided by Indian trails and rock cairns pointing the way to water. Here, at a small spring, are boulders inscribed with names and dates. Among the more decipherable are those of Weston and Hitchens.[14] After recrossing the Argus Range they followed up on some promising mineral signs missed before and established the "Coso Gold and Silver Mining District" that was to boom later in the '60s.

☆　☆　☆

Normally one would not pause to lengthily "footnote" the naming of Furnace Creek. But it exemplifies the hazy and oft frustrating endeavors to pin things down.

That Mormons, mining at Potosi to the southeast, had ventured into Death Valley is doubtful indeed. The LDS church, meticulous in their research and records have no evidence of it. Chalfant suggests that Mexican prospectors may have done so. Hanks also reports that there were Mexican miners in that area. It would certainly not be an impossibility. The lure of gold and silver knew no boundaries for the itinerant and adventurous drifting to and fro across the border.

Vying with the ore furnaces theory is that of crediting the

---

[14]Also see pages 32-33.

naming to the furnace like heat in the summer. C. B. Glasscock, of nearby Greenwater *Chuckwalla* fame, asserts, "A great deal of digging in dusty records has been done by some students of history to prove that the creek was so named because of the Darwin French party finding the remains of an ore smelting furnace in the wash. The evidence unearthed is extremely tenuous. In contrast, the July day of 1860 on which the Darwin French party first wallowed in that water was definitely hot. They named it 'Furnace Creek'." Historian Edwin Gudde agrees that "Probably so named because of the extreme heat . . . the tradition that Mormons built a furnace there in the 1850's to extract lead from galena, is apparently without foundation." P. T. Hanna, editor of *Touring Topics*, later *Westways*, and an eminent authority on California history and place names, fence straddles both theories.

Lts. Wheeler, Lyle, Birnie and Bendire who traversed the area a little later do not report any ore furnaces, although the small crude stone "furnaces" could have been missed or disappeared into indistinguishable rubble.

Rather surprisingly it is Manly who adds two closing, somewhat conflicting items. One is in recalling Travertine Springs:

> The little faint stream where we camped has since been named Furnace Creek. It was named in 1862 by some prospectors who built what was called an air furnace to reduce some ore found nearby, which they supposed to be silver but I believe it turned out to be lead and too far from transportation . . .

Then, as if to prove the failings of memory, Manly tells of one of his early '60s mining trips with Bennett, in which they found some promising ore in the Panamints:

> To prove its value, Bennett proposed to go to a high point and build an air furnace, such as we used to make in the lead mines of Wisconsin . . . when this was well tried and the ore would not melt [we] were jubilant and believed we had enough to make the whole company rich.

Ostensibly this was at Anvil Spring in southwestern Death

Valley. But in a *Pioneer* article of August 15, 1893, Manly says that while an attempt was made to melt the ore here, they moved their furnace building efforts to Furnace Creek, thus originating the name.

To the old gaming tables cry of "Place yer money and take yer chances" you can place your chips on heat or ore furnace, be it by Mormons, Mexicans, forgotten miners, Dr. French, even Manly, or just later theories.

Dr. George

In October of 1860, following closely on the trail of Dr. French, another party set out, including:

Dr. Samuel Gregg George	Henry O'Hara
Dr. W. B. (H.?) Lilley[15]	Moses Thayer
Wm. Henderson	J. R. Bill (Bell?)
Stephen Gregg	

After entering Death Valley they camped for three weeks near "Jayhawkers Well." According to State Mineralogist Hanks' report:

> They followed the same general route of the French Party, remaining at the Emigrant Camp for some time, prospecting the hills in every direction. At a locality two miles distant from a camp at "Hunter's Point"[16] they found water . . . and 12 miles distant a fine spring . . .
>
> Although ten years had passed, the tracks of men, women and children were distinctly seen, as fresh as if newly made; the irons of the wagons were where they had been left. The remains of ox yokes were seen, which had been laid out for use on the following day, and the chains extended on the ground in front of each wagon, showing the number of oxen to each, and traces of the old campfires were plainly seen . . .

---

[15] A "Lilley" is also listed with the Dr. French party. He may have missed leaving with them after rostered and joined Dr. George's group, possibly hoping to catch up. A slight difference in initials (W.B./W.H.) is noted as well as now being designated "Dr."

[16] Hunter Mountain in the northeast end of Panamint Valley is named for Zeb Hunter, an early settler and cattleman of the area.

Plenty of ducks, small birds and jack-rabbits were observed. While prospecting the hills, Dr. George and Mr. Thayer found the bones of white men within 300 yards of a spring of good water, believed to be of the emigrant party . . .

Seeing ducks, common to the large pools along Salt Creek, is far more understandable than the bones, questionably identified as those of white men, although the conclusion may have been based on remnants of clothing.

In returning the party followed an Indian trail through a pass in the mountains, finding and naming Wild Rose Spring, where they camped for two weeks of prospecting. Also in Emigrant Canyon they found Emigrant Spring, which they called Marble Spring.

While the Gunsight eluded them they did discover a deposit of antimony on Christmas Day 1860. Appropriately christened The Christmas Gift Lode, it was the first mining claim to be located in the Panamints.

They also made news in another way, not included in Hanks' Report. In the *Panamint City News* of March 23, 1875, Dr. George recalled:

W. T. Henderson and myself made a trip in the Slate Range . . . and fell in with William Alvord and a Mr. Manley[17] of San Jose, also a party of 16 men from Los Angeles in search of his (Alvord's) leads.[18] We left the party where we found them, but before leaving the party Alvord tried to show me where his lost lead was. From where we stood he pointed out the middle one of the high mountain peaks back of the Panamints and he described the lead as being within five miles from said peak.

36 days after parting with Alvord and his party, in passing Indian Wells we (again) found Alvord and Manley. They had lost their

---

[17] Manly is sometimes spelled Manley, including his by-lined series "From Vermont to California" in the *Santa Clara Monthly*, 1887-90. Also, although recorded in the family Bible as L. W. Manly ("and was always called Lewis") his headstone in the little cemetery at Woodbridge, Calif. reads William L. Manly.

[18] Who the 16 were is unknown. Manly doesn't say. Chances are they were a separate group following Manly and Alvord hoping they would lead them to the find, perhaps catching up briefly before going their own way.

horses and were out of every article of provisions. Alvord was sick with an abcess on his thigh and Manley was sustaining himself and Alvord on jack-rabbits.

Our party, having enough bread to sustain the sick man until our arrival in Kingsville, we put him on my riding horse and took him in. Alvord was afterwards killed by a man named Jackson because he could not show him the rich gold lead near Panamint.

Dr. George was another not easily discouraged. On April 1, 1861 the "Rough & Ready Mining Company" was formed at Visalia, with a roster that included:

A. H. Clark, *President*
Thomas Baker, *Secretary*
Dr. S. G. George, *Treasurer*
Dennis Searles (later of Searles Lake/Trona fame)
Robert Bailey (with French in 1860)
Thomas D. Baird

Also in his *Panamint News* article he tells that on this trek:

In addition to our first party was added six more men—J. R. Bell, J. W. Rolf, William Waters and others. After leaving Visalia we fell in at Walker's Pass with the "New World Mining & Exploring Company" under Col. W. P. Russ.

Little is known of this Spring trek except that they entered the Coso region and formed the Telescope Mining District. Although it is doubtful that they ventured beyond Panamint Valley, individual members may have, but of their wanderings there is no record.

Chapter Five

MANLY'S RETURN

Despite vowing that Death Valley had seen the last of him, Manly was to return at least twice.

Early in 1860 Bennett had returned to Death Valley with a party of five or six including William Alvord and some Mormons to search for the Lost Gunsight. While they did not find it they did find some silver near Anvil Spring in Butte Valley. Here, at Bennett's instigation, a crude air furnace was built with "jubilant results", and later moved to Furnace Creek.

Returning to Los Angeles they sent their samples to San Francisco for assay. The report indicated more lead than silver. And mindful of the difficult terrain and transportation the possible pay-off was deemed poor. But—Alvord had quietly pocketed an ore sample "nearly as dark as stone coal and speckled with gold!"

The secret leaked out and Alvord was persuaded to return with the company later that year. But, as with most "lost mines", Alvord couldn't relocate it. Or professed not to, saying "The snow was lower down on the mountains and the country appeared very different." Incensed, the others proposed to hang him. Finally they decided to leave him "to starve to death" and drove off with no one except Bennett saying "Goodbye".

Despite this conscience easing touch it seems one of the incongruities of man that Bennett, who should have been so mindful of the golden rule, would abandon another in the very area from which he and his family had been rescued.

Possibly it did bother him. After talking it over with a "Stockton",[19] three men—Bennett, Manly and a man named Twitchell—decided to rescue Alvord. Ruefully Manly comments:

> . . . when I concluded that it was my duty to go once again to Death Valley, to save and relieve as good a man as ever lived, from starvation, it seemed that I was born for the unwelcome task of rescuing the unfortunate of that terrible valley. But this man must be saved. We would follow on our '49 trail . . .

Before leaving they talked to '49er John Goller who had supposedly also found gold in the Death Valley area and which they may have linked with Alvord's discovery.[20]

In an interesting retracing of the '49er trail, their route was via the "Willows Camp" near Red Rock Canyon, Providence Springs in Etcharren Valley and the site of Fisch's body, and into Panamint Valley at Redlands Canyon. But perhaps mindful of its rock falls they continued farther up Panamint Valley to a canyon descriptive of Surprise Canyon.[21] Here Alvord appeared, having followed their mule tracks to camp!

Winter was setting in. Supplies were low. At least they had found a canyon with water and wood. While Alvord prospected and Manly hunted, Bennett and Twitchell took all of the animals and set out for supplies— and never returned!

Understandably Manly was embittered:

> I helped to save Bennett and others from starvation in Death Valley and why he left Alvord and myself to perish seemed strange. When I met Twitchell at Santa Monica in 1892 the first question I asked him was why he and Bennett had left us to starve.

Twitchell's explanation was that they had struggled for seven or eight days through heavy snow before reaching Los Angeles. By then a six week storm left so much snow as to make the

---

[19] Stover, in his narrative, reports that after catching up with Hunt, "I left a sack of clothes, the only valuables I had left, with a man by the name of Stockton from Tipton, Iowa."

[20] A letter dated Nov. 23, 1860, in the Armstrong Collection, notes they were to leave the following Monday as a party of three, to be joined by two others in search of Goller's gold.

[21] Site of Panamint City's 1873 silver discoveries.

mountains impassible. And they decided that by the time they could get back Manly and Alvord would have either starved or left the Panamints on their own.

Manly says, "It required some grace to become reconciled but we finally forgave them." But one can understand and sympathize with Manly's thoughts over the similar situation he and Rogers faced in '50 and the decision of Bennett and Twitchell ten years later.

While there has been some confusion over which of Dr. George's two mining trips they encountered Manly and Alvord, deductively it was the one in the winter of 1860-61 with Henderson. Dr. George's party was still in the Panamints when they found their antimony ore on Christmas Day, a timing that ties in with Twitchell's story of heavy snowfalls.

Manly's accounts of his mining experiences, appearing in various articles and letters, do contribute a certain confusion in separating one from another. And he does not tell of the first meeting with Dr. George in the Panamints. Only that after he and Alvord, lamed by a "boil on the knee" finally made their way to the base of the Sierra, they met five or six men, including Dr. George and "a Mormon named Jackson," with horses and mules, on their way back to Visalia.[22]

> They were acquaintances of Alvord; had found him two months before in the Death Valley country and had camped together.[23] They had also been out to locate a piece of Alvord's reported discovery. They were his friends and were willling to walk and let him ride. They gave us bread and meat and we went through Walkers Pass to the Kern River.

By now Manly should well have had it. But in March of 1861

---

[22] There is an intriguing possibility of this being the same Mormon named Jackson who was a partner of Bellerin' Tex at Greenland Ranch (now Furnace Creek Ranch) who had been run off by him at the point of a gun.

[23] Rather than another and unknown trip, a bit of memory slippage to which few are immune. Dr. George, 15 years later, recalled it as 36 days before and that he had met Alvord and Manly both times. Manly on the other hand seems to recall only the understandably more impressionable second meeting.

Alvord solicited his help in yet another attempt to find his rich discovery. This time they started out with a Dave Hickman, via Walker Pass and Little Lake as far as the Coso mines. Here Hickman returned to San Jose while Manly and Alvord remained at Coso where they heard of the outbreak of the Civil War. Since that event was in April 1861, and allowing time for word to reach remote Coso, it was now acceptably late May or June. And Manly reports storing some provisions with the Rough & Ready Mining Company, who had left Visalia with Dr. George in April.

Manly's success at Coso was probably so-so, for about the first of July they decided to make another Panamint search for Alvord's rich discovery[24] but ". . . were talked out of it because of the heat and Indians apt to be encountered."

Propositioned by other prospectors who promised to join them to make up a sufficiently large party for protection in the Fall, Manly and Alvord returned to the Sierra to hunt and relax. Shortly after they abandoned the Panamint project—Manly going to San Francisco and Alvord reportedly murdered by Jackson whom they had met at Indian Wells with Dr. George.

Ah! The interweaving of the threads of Fate! Manly and Rogers had met Dr. French near the San Fernando Mission back in January of 1850 on their rescue trek. Later, '49ers Turner and Toun triggered Dr. French's interest in the Gunsight. Now Dr. George, in a similar searching, chances upon Manly, one of the prime participants in the '49er saga with all of the coincidence of ships meeting in a vast uncharted ocean. One can also muse over the coincidence of Dr. George's "Rough & Ready Mining Company" and Chalfant's Gunsight-claiming Dr. McCormick in the mining camp of Rough & Ready.[25] And that Lillard, with Dr. French in 1861, was from nearby Oroville.

It can indeed be a small world.

---

[24] Interestingly, while the Panamints are best know for silver, rich pockets of gold have been found in a number of the canyons from Anvil Spring to Skidoo, an area where Alvord could have found his gold speckled specimen.

[25] Which laid a claim to fame by legendarily seceding from the Union as the Republic of Rough & Ready, over a quarrel with the Post Office.

Chapter Six

THE MAP MAKERS

DURING THE DECADE following the '49ers, familiarity with Death Valley was usually based on rumors, vague reports and hazy recollections. But in the 1860's a new breed of men appeared on the scene—the map makers. And maps by their very nature have an aura of factualness. Not that the first mappings were infallible by any means. Sometimes crude, with place-names tending to differ from map to map, they nevertheless exhibited a care given to black and white evidence that could be scrutinized, supported or criticized by others. Such as the first such map, that of Colonel Washington's San Bernardino Meridian Survey of 1854-55, viewed as suspect by many, perhaps unfairly so.[26]

Farley Map

In 1861, M. H. Farley's map of the "Newly Discovered Tramontane Silver Mines appeared, the first known to map Death Valley by name.

Farley had been a member of Dr. French's party the year before. Although his map shows Daylight Pass and the "Amargosa Mines" near Saratoga Springs in their acceptable locations, it also raises some doubt.[27] For example, it shows a "McCormack Well," near the site of Old Stovepipe Well, purportedly found and named by a Hugh McCormack in March 1861. State Min-

---

[26]See page 31 for detailing.

[27]The map covers from Sacramento to San Diego, a scope not only beyond that of Dr. French's party but, in all practicality, that of Farley's personal experiences. Doubtless it was put together from other sources as well.

eralogist Hanks' 1883 report tells that McCormack continued:[28]

> ... six miles south of these wells (to where) he met with a spring which emitted sulphuretted hydrogen gas. Here the old wagons of the emigrants were found. At Mesquite Springs he saw the shallow grave of a person supposed to be one of the emigrants, probably a woman, as a portion of a calico dress was found with the bones left exposed by the drifting of the desert sands ...

That no female '49er had perished in Death Valley does not rule out that a discarded calico dress may have been found by Indians and scraps of it abandoned later. And the bones may have been a titilating embellishment. But the locale of the wagon remains and the reference to Mesquite Springs are sound, as well as his inferential location of Bennett's Well.

Still, Hanks is inclined to be fanciful and repeat stories he had been told, without inclination or opportunity for confirmation. Adding to the mystery of McCormack Well and Farley's mapping of it is that the map was copyrighted in 1861. Seemingly it had to be drawn well before that. Either Farley had acquired the information between the return of the 1860 French party and McCormack's visit in 1861, simply adding it at the last minute, or the McCormack dating should be earlier than '61. Were McCormack and McCormick, who had been there in 1850 according to Chalfant, one and the same? Was the naming simply one of confusion over similar names? It is unlikely that one will ever know beyond all shadow of doubt.

1861 Boundary Survey ✔

In many ways the "1861 Boundary Survey Party" was one of the most qualified and notable early groups to explore Death Valley. Assuredly it was unique for its use of camels!

Early in 1860 joint plans were made by the United States and the State of California to survey the heretofore vague boundary

---

[28]Possibly a confusion of similarity of names with Dr. Wm. McCormick (see p. 27) although doubtful since the good doctor had married and hung out his M.D. shingle by 1860.

between California and the Territory of Nevada. A "Lieutenant" Sylvester Mowry was appointed Federal Commissioner to run the boundary,[29] with Lt. J. C. Ives the official astronomer.

Reaching San Francisco, November 1, 1860, Mowry found that California had repealed its authorization for the project. Despite this he sent one group to San Diego under Ives, while another assembled in Los Angeles. The Ives party proceeded to Fort Yuma, thence by steamer up the Colorado to Fort Mohave* near Needles. Apparently neither Ives nor Mowry accompanied them. And the Los Angeles contingent evidently only made a trip with supplies to the Ives camp on the Colorado.

Improvising on the original plan to survey the boundary from the 35th to 39th parallels, a reconnaissance party was formed to explore the general area, under Dr. J. N. Owens of Oroville and including:

James Hitchens	— (both with the French Party
J. H. Lillard	of 1860)
Joel Brooks	— guide
Richard "Dick" James	— interpreter
Sam McClelland	— ("who had been in Death Valley last spring prospecting", per the *Sacramento Daily Union*, 7/11/'61
Andrew Deming (Demming?)	
F. Biesta	— geologist and mineralogist
J. M. McLeod (McLoud?)	— astronomer
John S. Birdsall	
Aaron Van Dorn	— assistant surveyor
H. N. Jennings	
O. Hutton	

---

[29] Although resigned from the army in 1858, Mowry was still addressed by his former rank. Perhaps the finest account of this party is in Arthur Woodward's excellent *Camels and Surveyors in Death Valley*, 1961.

*Erwin Gudde's *California Place Names* (Univ. of Calif. Press) indicates the spelling of *Mojave* and *Mohave* "appears with more spelling variants than any other Indian name in California." However, the U.S. Board on Geographic Names, established Dec. 23, 1891, determined "the spelling Mojave for the California names in the Great Basin but left the spelling Mohave for the names on the Colorado (River), thus accentuating the difference in the origin and application of the two name clusters, despite their common source."

——— Hyer
Fritz (first name? nickname?)
Charles, a turk (or Charles A. Turk?)
Hadji Ali

The latter three were in charge of three camels, 22 to 24 mules, two or three horses and supplies for 60 days.

The accounts of the trek appeared in a series of articles in the *Sacramento Union* (June 25, 29, July 9, 11, 13, 31, August 7 and 10, 1861) with their authorship attributed to Hitchens.

Leaving their Colorado River camp February 13, 1861, the party proceeded to the Potosi Mines southwest of Las Vegas, Resting Springs and then northwest to where, on March 3rd:

> Two or three miles from camp we crossed the faint trail of some emigrant wagons driving to the southwest, made in the year 1849 by a party on their way to California who separated on the Salt Lake road from a very large train coming that route, and attempted to get in this way near the 36th parallel. They drove through the pass in the Amargosa Mountains above described and down Furnace Creek into Death Valley where they lost their animals and several of the company from exhaustion, from which incident the valley derives its name.

And, he adds, indicating the interest and exaggerations of the story that had swept the West:

> Their story has attracted considerable attention among the miners of California from the fact that they spread the report that in their rambling in this region they came across great quantities of native silver, some pieces so massive that they could not be overturned, and from which they made gunsights and other implements.

Although the article of July 11 is in error regarding "several" emigrants lost with the '49ers in Death Valley, it is one of the earliest appearances of the name Death Valley in print.[30] Interestingly, too, is the ready use of the name "Furnace Creek," although seemingly it was so named only a year before, possibly by Hitchens or Lillard while with Dr. French.

---

[30] It was preceeded in the *San Francisco Alta*, April 12, 1861.

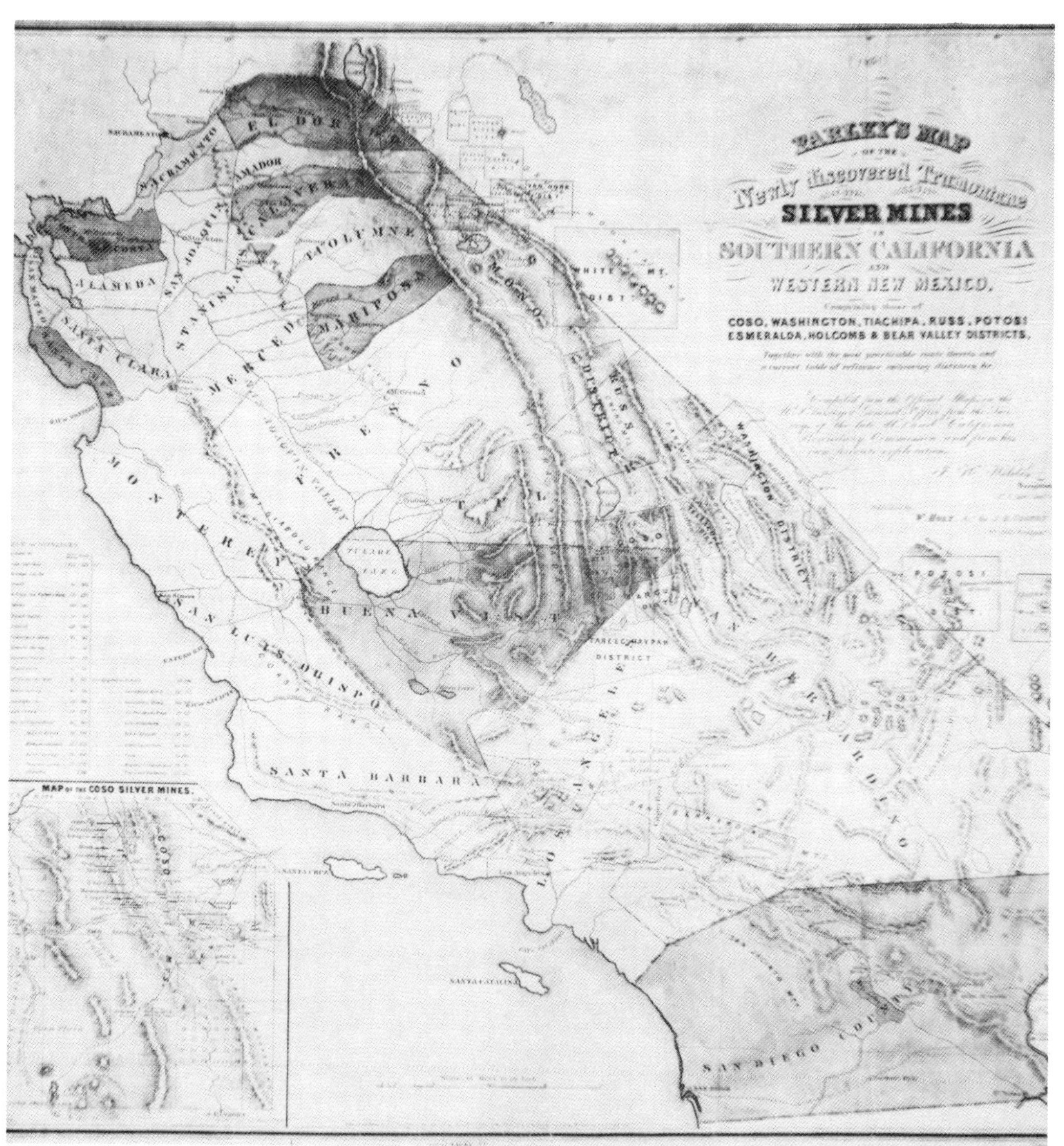

Farley's Map 1861

But the Boundary Party did not follow the emigrant trail into Furnace Creek. Instead, they continued northward to the vicinity of Beatty. Near here two of the men, McClelland and Deming, took off into Death Valley in search of water. Upon their failure to return the rest followed their trail ". . . to the summit where the ground became so rocky we lost all further signs" and descended into Death Valley. Indicatively this was via Echo Canyon for they wended a rough and winding way:

> . . . some three or four miles above its mouth or entrance into Death Valley. Some half mile below the junction (with Furnace Creek Wash) we came to the large spring we were in search of, or rather a series of springs [on] the right bank of the creek.

Obviously guided by Hitchens and Lillard who had been there before, they had reached Travertine Springs. Exploring in this vicinity they noted:

> Riding along the border of the plain we observed faint tracks of the emigrant wagons of '49 . . . and came to a spot where they had camped. . . . It was strewn with relics of their wagons—the spokes, tires and hubs of the wheels, and the iron of the running gear, chain, broken pots and other remains of camp equipage marking the abandonment and destruction of part of the train.

They then continued along "a very salty creek . . . some three miles and camped in a mesquite grove . . . containing a shallow well of very salty water"—

> Here again we found the traces of the emigrant encampment, bones of cattle in plenty and the less perishable parts of their abandoned wagons, trace chains, broken pots, etc.

And repeats the obsessive story, albeit with a dash of cold water:

> It was in searching for a pass through the Panamint Mountains that they were reported to have made the rich silver discovery . . . which if not exactly all talc came very near it being as we proved [that] their silver at least all talc, a shining white mecaeous stone having much the appearance of silver.

Whatever their skepticism over the silver, their finding of two separate '49er camps a few miles apart does support one being at McLean Spring and another, that of Sheldon Young's contingent, near Midway Well.

The reconnaissance party, in Death Valley seven days, took stock of their supplies and jaded animals and decided to head for Walker Pass via Towne Pass. But soon after they progressed into the latter they branched off into a spur canyon:

> Town's Pass, a gap through the Panamint Mountains into the next basin to the west, and on the direct route from Death Valley to Owens Lake, was directly before us . . . but this we left and entered the mountains up a wide arroyo . . . for three miles [and] camped at a very small hole of water . . . around which are growing some reeds and a few tufts of bunch grass and which is known as Hitchen's Spring.

By no small coincidence the small spring, since renamed Jayhawker Spring, is marked by a group of boulders inscribed with ancient petroglyphs and an array of names and initials including "J. Hitchens 1860." In bypassing or missing the actually less evident entrance to Emigrant Canyon, Hitchens had guided them to water found in Dr. French Party scoutings. In so doing he would be providing this party with some reassurance that he knew whereof he spoke, with the obvious evidence of having been there before.

From this spring the party ascended the arroyo to its crest. Crossing the rather steep ridge at its head they apparently missed the cluster of small springs just to the east (Burro, Burns, Willow, Green, Canyon and Malpai Springs) as they continued into another arroyo, climbing to nearly 7000' before descending into White Sage Flat.

Here the party separated. Biesta and three others were left at a spring while the rest circled south, west, then northwest to the Coso mines via Darwin Canyon and on to Owens Lake.

Of their trail across and out of Death Valley there is no known

Hitchens Spring, since renamed Jayhawker Spring, in a spur canyon between Towne Pass and Pinto Peak. Boulders bear inscriptions of petroglyphs (note small rock cairn trail signs of water) and prospectors, including Hitchens and Weston with the French Party of 1860. Adjoining is that of '49er "W.B.R(ood)".

map. But as a survey-exploration party their account is more authoritative than most to this time, its purpose more factual than prospector wanderings.

Bancroft Map ✔

In 1864 another map appeared—Bancroft's map of "California, Nevada, Utah, Arizona." Showing "Death Valley," Furnace Creek, and *McCormick* Spring at old Stovepipe Well, it evidences a gaining knowledge of the area.

Buel - Todd ✔

Up to now most of the early Death Valley explorations were of California origin. However, stimulated by the Comstock and Reese River discoveries, the fledgling Pahranagat mines near Pioche, and quixotically, the excitement over the Lost Breyfogle Gold, David Buel (spelled equally with one "l" or two) and Joseph Todd led a small party from Austin, Nevada, in January 1864 for:

> . . . the purpose of searching for a mine reputed to be fabulously rich, found by three survivors of the ill-fated immigrant train of 1852 and for general prospecting.

The year 1852 is typical of the loose and varied dating of the period. No less an authority than J. Ross Browne, in his 1869 *Adventures in Apache Land,* used the same dating in repeating a tale that has been in the telling for many years.

According to the *Reese River Reveille,* October 2, 1865, the Buel-Todd party proceeded to the Spring Mountains and Las Vegas, returning via Death Valley:

> Here they found the remains of the unfortunate train. The iron works of eight wagons, which had doubtless been burned by Indians—gunlocks, trunk locks and hinges, broken glass and earthenware were lying scattered on the ground. Wells that had been dug nearby contained poisonous water as the numerous bones of animals but too well attested.

Buel-Todd Map 1864-65

In all probability they had found the 1849 Jayhawker camp at McLean Spring. But the water, while brackish, was hardly poisonous. The animals had been deliberately killed for their meat, and the wagons burned to dry that meat and possibly for warmth and firelight.

The article, perhaps feeling the party's return from such a forbidding region was sufficient accomplishment, does not tell more of the return to Austin. However, from the map that combines both the Buel-Todd trek and that of Todd the following year, they apparently managed to reach the Pahranagat mines near Pioche for some of the trails are identified as "Mr. Welton-Buel Route."

CHAPTER SEVEN

TODD, BLASDEL & BREYFOGLE!

STILL INTENT ON The Lost Gunsight, Joseph Todd returned to Death Valley, leaving Austin on February 25, 1865:[31]

> ... in search of the locality of some rich silver lodes discovered by the party that made the disastrous passage of Death Valley in 1852. The only present survivor of that party is a lady, living now in Santa Clara County, California, who has in her possession some exceedingly rich specimens of ore containing native silver.

With no information to counter it, the 1852 dating is repeated. But their tracing the silver specimens to one of the '49er women is intriguing, and typical of the rumors that surrounded that episode. Certainly many of the '49ers survived beyond 1865, including Manly who died in 1903, Mrs. Brier in 1913, Colton in 1919, and Stephens, "the last of the Jayhawkers" in 1921. Be that as it may, Buel did not return with Todd[32] in this small party of five that included Todd, Hardy Bonner, Wm. Gearhart, Edward Gillman and one unnamed.

Excerpts from 1865 items in the *Reese River Reville* report the group retraced the 1864 route through Smoky Valley to Silver Peak and Lida Valley, then veered to enter Death Valley from the north on March 13:

> Some springs were found in the cluster of sand hills in the middle of the northern end of the valley.... These are [now] called "Desert Spring". From there down a deep arroyo for 18 miles

---

[31] *Reese River Reveille*, April 24, 1865.

[32] Scattered references to David Buel indicates his continuance in early Nevada mining activities including representing the Reese Mining District in Paris in 1867. But of Joseph Todd nothing more is known.

they reached "Bonners Spring" marked on Bancroft's map as "McCormick Spring".[33] Here they remained prospecting for two days. A southerly journey of 35 miles brought them to Buel's Well, dug by Buel's party last year. The water is salt and alkalied but necessity compelled its use. This is at the head of the salt marsh in Death Valley and is 12 miles north of the remains of the "lost wagons" of 1852. The bones of the cattle of that unfortunate expedition lie around this water in great quantity.

A subsequent article in the *Reese River Reveille*, September 11, 1865, elaborates on the Todd passage from Mount Magruder near Lida:

> Winding down this way about 20 miles . . . the head of the valley is reached at the junction of two canyons which form it.[34] At this point there are numerous springs, all tainted with alkali. . . . What appears to be a river bed runs through the center of the valley [for] a distance of 35 miles. Passing down the valley some 10 miles farther we came upon the vast salt marsh. It was at this point that a large party of immigrants suffered severely in 1852 and it is now known as "Lost Wagons". The iron work of many wagons are still to be seen, and many other articles are occasionally found by adventurous explorers. It is generally believed that some of the immigrants perished although it is not known to be the fact.

Proceeding southeasterly to "Gearhart's Spring,"[35] then northeasterly about 30 miles to "Summit Spring"[36] on the eastern slopes, the reports of this party end on a historical high-note:

> . . . they had fallen in with a party from Smoky Valley composed of Messrs. Breyfogle, E. T. Martin, A. A. Simonds, G. W. Cloud and McKinistry. These were in search of some gold bearing quartz lodes that Mr. Breyfogle had found on a previous

---

[33] The name and location shift with the telling. At times it is called McCormick's, others as McCormack; sometimes placed near "Surveyors Well" and "Grapevine Springs," other times at Old Stovepipe Well and McLean Spring. In the Todd account it was well to the north per their logging some 47 miles to signs of an emigrant camp.

[34] Approximating Oriental Wash and Grapevine Canyon north of Scotty's Castle.

[35] Perhaps found by Gearhart, a member of the party, and named by or for him. Their map indicates it at or near Travertine Springs.

[36] Probably Keane or Hole in the Rock Spring near Daylight Pass.

expedition. The precise nature of what the company found is not disclosed but it is sufficient to induce them to return. Mr. Breyfogle was left with two months supplies of provisions to hold the place and prospect during the absence of the others. The party will return immediately and we expect shortly to hear of a far richer district than is even Reese River or Silver Peak.

It is not clear just where the Todd party encountered Breyfogle, although likely in the Funeral or Grapevine ranges. Lending credence to this is that the Blasdel Expedition of 1866 also met Breyfogle in this vicinity.

Tempting as it may be to delve into the story of Breyfogle's fabulously rich gold, it is a tale already told many times.[37] Suffice to say in reminder, Breyfogle had been found delirious near Stump Spring in the Amargosa, clutching some reddish rocks gleaming with gold. By the time he recovered he had forgotten just where he found the ore. It was to be another legendary lost lode to rival the Gunsight!

As an inspiration to those seeking to succeed where others have failed it is irresistable to add a wild but plausible possibility. In one of the most seldom seen areas of the lonesome lands bordering Death Valley, not far from Tippipah Springs in the present AEC Test Site, is an unusual obelisk-boulder inscribed "BY FOGLE 1863." A prank? Perhaps. Was "BY" a contraction of "Byron?" (see footnote [#37]). But there it stands, amid distinctive brick-red outcroppings so identified with Breyfogle's gold samples that purportedly assayed $100,000 a ton!

At least some of the Todd party were more than a little interested, for Gearhart was to join Simonds of the Breyfogle party in the searching, either remaining behind or returning after the Todd group reached Austin via Pahranagat.

While there have been rumors and fleeting references to an

---

[37] Superbly told in Harold Weight's *Lost Mines of Death Valley*, which also establishes Breyfogle's first name as Charles (C.C.), not Jacob. And in another variance is named Byron W. Fogle.

"Byfogle 1863" inscription

official record of the Buel-Todd explorations, it has yet to be found. However, the *Reveille* of October 2, 1865 reported:

> Mr. Todd was unsuccessful in the main object of his search but his explorations will prove of great value to the public from the geographical and topographical knowledge obtained. This information will soon be given the public in a large and handsomely executed map.

Fortunately the map did surface and is one of the best early maps of the Death Valley area. Obviously and authoritatively done from on the scene knowledge it also shows Death Valley and Furnace Creek by name. Titled "Map of the Reese River Mining Districts, Showing Explorations of D. E. Buel in 1864 and Joseph Todd in 1865" it was "Compiled by John Todd (son? brother?), Drawn by E. W. Welton." While the latter was not with Todd he evidently was with Buel for some of the trails are identified as "Mr. Welton-Buel Route 1864."[38]

Published by "D. Van Nostrand, 192 Broadway, N.Y.," it bears a helpful line that it was "Entered according to Act of Congress in the year 1866 . . . in the District Office of the United States for the Southern District of New York." But copies had obviously been circulated in the Fall of 1865 per map-printed endorsements of its authenticity. Dated October and November 1865, they are by Major General Rosecrans; *Reveille* Editor B. J. Burns; J. Slauson, Mayor of Austin; mining engineer A. Blatchly; and Lander County Surveyor M. J. Noyes, in general agreement that it was "the only correct map extant."

Blasdel Expedition

The Silver Boom was on! Austin, Pioche, Belmont, Hiko, Tem Piute, the Mt. Irish mines, and a host of others were in full swing to the sound of picks, stamp mills, blasting powder and gunfire to the deadly tune of a man-a-day overtures. But they were new, isolated camps with little known of the country between.

---

[38] While the *Reveille* articles do not indicate Todd's return route, well defined trails on the map show they did so via the Amargosa and the Pahranagat.

As the first Governor of the almost two year old State of Nevada, H. G. Blasdel was hardly in need of a politico's prerogative of hitting the hustings for votes when he headed south on a roundabout route to the Pahranagat Mining Districts around Pioche in the Spring of 1866.[39] For one thing, there were scarcely enough constituents there to warrant a long and rugged trip through the little known region. For that matter, few were at all sure just where the Pahranagat activities were. But evidently not one to designate the less desirable and perchance enviously adventurous task to others, the stalwart 6' 5" Blasdel personally headed "an expedition for the purpose of opening up direct communications between the settlements in the Pahranagat and the towns in the western portion of the state in the belief some nearer and more practicable route than the one by way of Egan Canyon and Austin must exist."

There are two accounts of this expedition—both written by the same man under two names and in notably different manners. One is the official account, appearing in the "Annual Report of the State Mineralogist of the State of Nevada" as "Appendix E, Journal of Explorations in Southern Nevada in the Spring of 1866 by His Excellency, Governor Blasdel of Nevada, by R. H. Stretch." The other is a less formal, more detailed and descriptive account that appeared as a series of 16 articles in the Virginia City *Territorial Enterprise* from March to May 1866. These were also written by State Mineralogist Stretch but as correspondent for the newspaper and signed "Viator."

While minor variances occur in the two versions, it is the more casual and elaborative *Enterprise* articles that are the most informative, with the Appendix E a reflective corroboration. Together they are one of the most descriptive and authoritative early accounts. Not only of routes and terrain, but of place names that flicker dimly from the past.

From Carson City the expedition proceeded south of Walker

---

[39] Coincidentally, in the next election his opponent was D. E. Buel, whom he defeated.

Lake to Montgomery—"laid out on quite an extensive scale but its inhabitants at present number about 10"—arriving March 26, 1866. They continued to the promising Silver Peak District, which inspired Stretch to write: "This is a great place, barren as a boarding house table after dinner but rich in curiosities of all sorts."

Here, if not already accompanied by them, they were joined by a cavalry detail. At least it is noted by:

> Messrs. Lambert, Schooling and others from Washoe left for the Kearsarge (mines) so that our party is reduced to 18 exclusive of the cavalry. We start in the morning for Pahranagat in a southeasterly direction. All are in good health and spirits. Some few wagons will go with us but the majority of the party are equipped with pack mules.

The composition of the "cavalry" and how far they accompanied is clouded. The Appendix E entry simply notes the Blasdel party comprised "over 20 individuals with a buggy and one wagon." But 16 names are culled from the articles:

H. G. Blasdel, *Governor*	——— Vandewater
"young Blasdel", his son	J. C. James
R. H. Stretch, *State Mineralogist*	——— Martin
Rev. A. F. White	George Ernst
Jerry Ripple	——— Day
G. Gillis	——— Cross
——— Butterfield[40]	——— a Mexican packer
W. "Sol" Lewis	Chauncey Noteware

—plus a W. Campbell and a Mr. McCall, who joined in Death Valley.

Leaving Silver Peak April 3, they arrived at Alida Valley Springs, 25 miles south, the second day. On April 5 they started for the Pahranagat but lost their way and returned to Alida Valley.

A little less jovial now, Stretch writes:

> As for the country beyond here, it is beyond description— desolate and barren as the suburbs of hell. The slowness of our

---

[40]Possibly Henry Butterfield, guide with Lt. Wheeler's 1869 expedition.

progress renders it necessary for Chauncey Noteware to leave us here, much to our regret, his official business not allowing him to be away as long as the trip was likely to take.

Possibly, too, it was a matter of discretion being the better part of valor. For in the same issue of the *Enterprise* there is a separate item by Blasdel:

> My faith is not very strong we can get through on this route on account of the great lack of water, but we will go on as far as our animals will stand it, and then when we can go no further and are compelled to abandon the enterprise we will do so, but until then our march is onward. If we find we cannot cross Death Valley with safety to ourselves and our animals we will seek some other road.

It is not only interesting that the name "Death Valley" seems well established by 1866, but that they were to traverse it, heading south, although the Pahranagat was far to the northeast. Perhaps it was, as announced, a matter of discovering a new and alternate route to the one from Austin. Or a decision to follow the tracks of Buel and Todd as a better choice than blazing a new and unknown way through a land "desolate and barren as the suburbs of hell."

The following detailing of their route may seem excessive, yet warranted for many reasons. It is the most authoritative of early accounts. The sites and scenes help to identify time-blurred locations and changing place names—a boon to those who would follow, however vicariously, in the footsteps of history. It records encountering Breyfogle. And it helps to pin down the story of Blasdel finding nine skeletons of the Savage-Pinney Party as fact or fiction. And, frankly, for the sheer enjoyment of Stretch's journalistic writing.

With all of this in mind, indulgently follow along as the Blasdel Expedition left Alida Valley on April 9, over "an old wagon trail"[41] part way to Desert Springs (Sand Springs, probably via Oriental Wash):

---

[41] Probably that of Buel and Todd (1864-65) although Silver Peak was stirring as

> . . . near the head of a long valley stretching away to the south-
> east as far as the eye can see and separated from Fish Lake Valley
> and its continuations by a high range of barren mountains. The
> springs are surrounded by low hills and have gradually built up
> a small mound. Water was abundant but grass scarce as money
> in the pocket of a bummer. We have received our last letters
> from home and henceforth cast off into the wilderness.

Sand Springs (Big and Little) is at a junction of canyon-routes used by countless prospectors over the years, although now little known in the risky going north of Scotty's Castle.[42] Since there is no further mention of the cavalry this may have been the point of parting.

On the 10th they arrived at "Bonner's Spring" (Grapevine Springs), named by or for Hardy Bonner with the Todd party in 1865. After a peaceful encounter with Indians, who had "made ponds in the foothills to lure passing ducks," they continued south-ward for about 18 miles when "it became painfully evident our trail had come to an end."

Due to Ripple's wagon breaking down, the group split. Blasdel and others stayed behind to help with repairs and to hunt for water. Others, including Stretch, went on to catch up with the packers who had gone ahead. About 30 miles from Bonner's Spring they found the pack train:

> . . . in a waste of sand hillocks, whither they had been tempted
> by some bright green locust trees which flourished even in that
> desolation. As the sun went down behind the hill we made camp
> with not a blade of grass and only a small canteen of hot water
> among a party of eleven.

The next day's explorations were rewarded by grass and a fine spring on the slopes to the east. Friday, only coincidentally

---

early as 1864 and prospectors may have started to range out and south toward Gold Mountain and the Last Chance Range of the northern Panamints. One can only spec-ulate how old the wagon trail may have been. Thought has been voiced it might have been Frémont's Fifth. However, so far as known, no wagons accompanied The Path-finder on this segment. Nor did the '49ers get this far north.

[42] Not to be confused with Sand Springs, a pivotal point on the '49er route, near Tem Piute north of the AEC area in Nevada.

the 13th, they "staid in camp, but as some of the party had fortunately found the lost trail, three horsemen have gone ahead to explore the route to Breyfogle's Springs, from which place, or Furnace Creek, you shall hear from me again."[43]

On Monday, the 16th, they left the spring on the slopes to where:

> . . . we met our scouts and under their direction finally crossed the eastern end of the sand hills . . . and found ourselves at Wilson's Wells, some 30 miles from the last camp.

By its elusive location and mysterious naming, "Wilson's Wells" deserves more than passing reference. A Wilson's Wells is found on an 1881 Nevada map, along an old stage route between Bare Mountain, Nevada, and Owens Lake, but so loosely located it could be interpreted as anywhere from Saline Valley to Mesquite Spring. The Von Schmidt-Gibbes map of 1869 shows it near Midway Well, about 15 miles north of McLean Spring.

But who was Wilson? And how was the naming known by Blasdel in 1866?

It may have been named by the Buel '64 party. Or the unnamed fifth man with Todd in '65. Or even one of the unlisted members of the Blasdel party. Certainly the knowledge of a water hole, and by name, in such a remote area would be credited to someone known more than the unpublicized inspiration of some wandering prospector.

About 1868, James Hobbs, however one may be dubious of this flamboyant soldier of fortune,[44] reports a Death Valley experience involving a William Wilson. And a William Wilson is officially credited with the Pine Grove discoveries at not too far away Aurora in 1866, and later found dead beside a Panamint Valley spring.

The *Inyo Independent*, in 1872, also reports a W. F. Wilson

---

[43] How, when and where they relayed reports back to the *Territorial Enterprise* is a mystery. Likely by assigned "messengers" who deserved more than anonymity.
[44] See page 86.

as operating a stage line from Carson to Aurora, as well as a W. B. Wilson; not to mention a John Wilson, active in Austin-Hamilton stage line operations in the 1860's. Then, too, there is a Tom Wilson, son-in-law of Panamint chieftan "Hungry Bill." And a B. D. Wilson, who came to California with the Workman-Rowland Party of 1841. Appointed sub-agent for Indian Affairs in 1857, it was noted that he was an old mountaineer, a veteran of Indian campaigns, and as having engaged in cattle and sheep drives from Southern California to the northern mines before 1852.

Add to these the name of Jonathan W. Wilson, an early day prospector who was better known as "Dirty Shirt" Wilson. And an A. D. Wilson, topographer with the Clarence King expedition of the late 1860's. Even a Charles Wilson, who was assuredly known to Blasdel who had appointed him Lincoln County Commissioner. Toss in a sprinkling of other Wilsons in the early boom days of Nevada, along with the Wilson for whom Mt. Wilson is named and who christened Big Bear Lake because its area was over-run with grizzlies[45] and you have a plethora of Wilsons providing prime possibilities.

History can indeed weave a snarled tangle of threads.

Enough of such digression and to continue with Blasdel's report.

> Wilson's Wells is about seven foot deep with several feet of good water. It is sunk in the middle of a small patch of inferior grass at the foot of the mountains on the east side of the valley, the meadow being depressed below the general level of the valley, the undulations of the sand hills to the west making it difficult to see when approaching from that direction.

It was at Wilson's Wells that the Indians raided Ripple's crippled wagon, taking "a sack of flour and about 40 pounds each of bacon and sugar." The loss, Stretch writes, "was a serious item in the state of our larder, but it was almost compensated by the

---

[45] Also credited to Benjamin D. Wilson, known as Don Benito in the Pueblo de Los Angeles.

amusement it raised at the expense of the ex-proprietor who had confidently asserted the Indians would never discover the treasure." Later he was somewhat less amused to report that "the only demi-john of whiskey in the company got badly busted away."

On April 17th they broke camp, traveling:

> . . . over heavy sand and mud flats, the crust of which would break like thin ice beneath our horses feet . . . some 15 miles to "Lost Wagons". The valley here widens out and gradually decreases in elevation. From the débris they appear to be chiefly limestone, slate and granite; and small fragments of metal bearing float rock would indicate the presence of metaliferous veins but the almost entire absence of timber and water will ever render even rich mines of no value. In many places the winds had piled the loose shifting sands into huge banks over the trail although but made a few months previously.

Here they were to find, and help to corroborate, a camp of the '49ers:

> Lost Wagons is the name given to some little pools of alkaline water near the north end of Death Valley,[46] named in memory of the early emigrants who, on account of their cattle giving out were obliged to abandon their wagons, the remains of which lie scattered around. . . . But few of that party are left to tell of that fearful journey; and these fragments of wood and iron speak more eloquently than words of the sufferings of those miserable wanderers who, footsore and weary, with thirst and starvation staring them in the face, were obliged to abandon their wagons, the remains of which lie scattered around their old camping grounds, and trust themselves to a country in which even the meanest of God's creatures can scarcely maintain a foothold.

> The Indians say they had no water for the last 80 miles[47] and that they had been compelled to throw away one article after another

---

[46] A "Lost Wagons" was once a mapped point northwest of Titus Canyon. But this is authoritatively traced to the abandonment of an early borax wagon. From Stretch's descriptions and the quantity of remains found his "north end of Death Valley" refers to the northern edge of the sink itself, extending south from the large sand dunes, and the remains either those of Sheldon Young's camp near Midway Well or the Jayhawkers at McLean Spring.

[47] Actually the '49ers had renewed water supplies at Travertine Springs, about a third of that distance.

in the vain hope of enabling their worn-out stock to reach water. What this country is in the summertime may be gathered from the fact that water is an article of trade among the Indians who, from their long residence, must be acquainted with all of the springs and water sources which are found within its limits.

Among so destitute a company it is more than likely that some of them perished at this place . . . but there were no monuments to show that any of them were buried there . . . and not knowing where we should find grass and water for our own stock we were compelled to hurry on after a very brief stay.

As with few, the Stretch accounts capture the desolation and deprivation faced by the '49ers. And he tells it well in his *Enterprise* version. While the Blasdel party had come from the north, and the '49ers from the east, the trails had crossed where the descriptive impact was similar:

Wending our way through a belt of low barren gravel hills we came in sight of the famous Death Valley which has gained so unenviable a reputation as the resting place of some member of almost every party that has tempted its desolation.

Very slowly indeed we skirted its northern limits, sometimes through heavy sands, sometimes over yielding alkalined earth and sometimes across broken gravel washes, til sunset overtook us. At that time we were close to the edge of the desert valley which spread out before us some forty miles to the south, an almost unbroken sheet of salt and alkali which glistened in the sunset like a beautiful sheet of water.

Ripple's wagon was unable to go any farther, having dragged the wagon with a wheel locked all day, and though there was nothing but a little dead salt grass and a few pools of water, too salty to drink, we had to turn out and make the best of the situation. During the day we found the tracks of white men and even that small link with civilization was some consolation.[48] Others, at any rate, were no better off than ourselves, and although some of our party were inclined to grumble, we slept as soundly as if we had been in our own beds in Virginia City.

---

[48] Either/or the Buel-Todd tracks, or a Breyfogle party. Possibly indicated by horse-mule droppings, camp discards or bootprints.

On Wednesday (April 18) they traveled three miles to "Brey-fogle Spring," perhaps near Nevares Spring, in one of the spur washes in the foothills, where "water and an inferior kind of grass were abundant."

Being at a loss as to our exact location, some of us went out the next day to examine the country to the southward while others ascended the mountains to the east for the purpose of getting a good view of the country. Both parties had a good view of Fur-nace Creek but the foothills were cut up with such impassable canyons where it was impossible to take a horse that we found it necessary to retrace our steps nearly to the level of the valley.

Noteworthy is that they did not cross the valley westward to where they were rumored to have found the bodies of nine of the Savage-Pinney party huddled behind a pile of brush. Nor is any mention made of such an incident. And certainly Stretch, in his role as reporter for the free-wheeling *Enterprise* was not apt to miss that newsy item.

On Friday, the 20th, they retraced their steps, striking out across low hills:

. . . which some of our party very aptly described as "self-rising" earth so much did its surface look like a batch of bread before baking, and reached Furnace Creek about noon. Following up an immense wash we entered a broad canyon, the long looked for pass to the eastward which was to take us to Pahranagat, and not one of us but felt a thrill of joy when we came to a stream of water. . .
Up the canyon we traveled, following a recent wagon track, by whom we could not tell. On either side the gravel bluffs were worn into the most fantastic shapes by the long continued action of wind and weather, while a fringe of willows and mesquite marked the course of the refreshing stream. Glad as we were to note these little incidents imagine our joy when we descried a party of white men camped a few hundred yards ahead, their horses grazing quietly down the canyon! They proved to be a party of enthusiastic prospectors headed by Mr. Breyfogle, who had made their way into the valley from the sink of the Mojave

in search of a fabulously rich gold mine which Mr. Breyfogle found about two years ago.[49]

Leaving "Hadley Springs"[50] on April 21, they made an abortive attempt to force passage over the rock strewn slopes and sandy washes toward the Amargosa. Turned back, six persisted in continuing east, including Lewis, Martin and Gillis:

> We left them with great regret, but as they had joined the expedition voluntarily they had a perfect right to leave it whenever they saw fit. They had with them an abundance of provisions and on dividing our remaining water, each man had about a pint and a half, sufficient with economy to last through the day.

The others returned to Furnace Creek where they found some members of the Breyfogle party that had just got into camp. These reported they had found a pass to the Amargosa but had been without water for two days.

Cheered by the former, concerned over the latter news, Blasdel hired a wagon and a large cask from the Breyfogle company, and with about 70 gallons of water set out after the six "should they need assistance and in case they were found to be alright to strike eastward in the hope of finding a trail running north to Pahranagat as we knew that parties had left Los Angeles with the intention of following that route."

The search party of five comprised the Governor, Rev. White, Jerry Ripple, W. Campbell and Mr. McCall, "the latter two belonging to the Breyfogle party." The others remained at Furnace Creek where, in the late afternoon of the following day, "Sol Lewis" came staggering into camp reporting the others were scattered along the road and one of them missing since Sunday night."[51]

---

[49] Encountered by Todd the year before, Breyfogle may also have been in the area in 1863 and 1864 as well.

[50] Named by Washington's "San Bernardino Meridian Survey" party of 1854, eventually renamed Travertine Springs.

[51] In the back and forth movements of searchers and sought, some may have been missed in the passings due to terrain or darkness. Or some may have entered Echo Canyon, a northeasterly route to the Amargosa, branching off of Furnace Creek Wash and used by miners in the Schwab-Lee mining booms.

> We met two of the party up the canyon. Some five miles further young Blasdel found Martin lying under a bank unable to go on and taking him into the buggy brought him into camp. His companion, Ernst of Dayton, had left him with the intention of reaching a small spring about six miles away and returning with water. But when we [the search party] reached that spring only his clothes were there, he having taken them off to walk more freely.
>
> It was now dark but we sent our Mexican packer, the best man in the company, to follow a trail to the spring. About 3 o'clock in the morning he returned, having found Ernst about 600 yards from the spring, completely exhausted and fast asleep.

The dissident six had reached Ash Meadows where they separated to look for water, losing Gillis in the process. The remaining five then returned, "losing five out of eight horses on the way." They reported searching, shouting and shooting but Gillis unfortunately had a "serious defect of hearing" and could not hear them to respond. Nor was he found by the Blasdel searchers.

The main group remained at Furnace Creek for 13 days, prospecting, recuperating and reconnoitering.

> Near this place we also found a small fire where a human being had been burned. Small fragments of bone and a few teeth inclined me to the belief they were Indian remains as this was their usual custom of disposing of their dead, but some in our party suggested they might belong to one of the unfortunate men who were killed here by Indians while prospecting for the Breyfogle ledge early last Fall. One piece of the skull certainly had the appearance of being fractured.

Upon the return of a small search party with disappointing news about Gillis, but good news about a way to Pahranagat, the expedition moved out:

> Six of the Breyfogle party decided to throw in their fortunes with ours, the remaining three returning to Los Angeles by the route they had followed into the valley.

Leaving May 7, they found:

> The grade up Furnace Creek is heavy, probably 100 feet to the mile . . . and when the summit was reached the team was so completely exhausted that a dry camp was inevitable. The party, however, had found a wagon track during the day, which was supposed to have been Buel's[52] and as there was no return track accompanying it the conclusion was pretty logical that it went to water . . .

After camping in Ash Meadows they continued eastward over a low ridge and on the flat dug and found water at six feet.

> The well was named Blasdel's Well, in honor of the Governor who suggested the idea and dug the well with his own hands.

However laudable it was somewhat of a needless effort for—

> May 10th. Six miles across meadow and sand flats, with a small white ash timber and grape vines brought us to a range of low coraline limestone hills with a fine spring on the summit, in a cave thirty feet long and ten wide.

Fatefully, historically, although not realizing it, they had reached a key point on the route of the Death Valleyites of 1849. The "fairy-like cave containing a spring with magnificent water" that Nusbaumer described. Certainly such caves with springs are rare, to the point of only one being known in that area—Devil's Hole, in the little island of Death Valley National Monument in Nevada, on the edge of Ash Meadows.

Proceeding approximately along the route of present day U.S. 95, the group continued to a little creek, "which is called Indian Creek," where they found fresh tracks of a wagon and a campfire still burning and which they "supposed was made by Day's party."

Day, a listed member of the Blasdel company, apparently had been sent ahead to Las Vegas for supplies:

> Day's wagon was overtaken about 15 miles from Las Vegas and though short himself, sufficient was obtained for present necessities with which Campbell and McCall returned to the Governor while Mr. Cross went with Mr. Day to Las Vegas.

---

[52] Or possibly Todd, with the Buel-Todd Party of 1864 and who returned in '65.

The "supply party" managed to secure "plenty of beef and mutton but very little flour as it was scarce in Las Vegas," and returned to Indian Creek.

From a flashback in a later article, written from Pahranagat, it seems that the Blasdel party divided, presumably after being re-supplied, with some proceeding to Pahranagat and others taking another look for Gillis. And they eventually found his body, about four miles from an isolated butte. There they buried him, marking the grave with a large mound. Ironically, in the digging they found "water running freely when we were scarcely two feet deep."

From Indian Creek (May 13), "the road lay almost due north up a long valley bordered on either side by barren mountains" (Indian Springs Valley) to Quartz Spring (near the northern end of the Pintwater Range) and about 57 miles farther arrived at Hatfield's Ranch[53] where:

> . . . so exhausted were the Governor and Mr. White that when the house and spring came in sight, though not more than 200 yards away, it took them half an hour to accomplish the distance, having to sit down and rest every few yards.

"We had lost," Stretch writes, "10 horses and mules on the trip but every member in spite of the physical discomforts of the journey was well, probably in better health than when they started." And he adds, laconically, "None of us, however, have any anxiety to repeat the experiment."

The final *Enterprise* article (#16, May 22, from Springer's Ranch[54]) concludes with a description of a tour of Coal Valley, Mt. Irish, Pahranagat Lake, Logan, Hiko and Crystal Springs. There were, he says, "one thousand locations on record with

---

[53] Shown on an 1881 Nevada map as just northwest of Mt. Irish and at the south end of Garden Valley, about 60 miles north of Quartz Spring. In Averett's *Directory of Southern Nevada Places Names*, Crescent City is listed as Hatfield's. Near here George Ernst of Blasdel's party was to locate the Freiburg mines not long afterwards.

[54] The Nevada 1881 map shows Springer's just around the hump of the Golden Gate Range, northeast of Hatfields and near the old Freiburg stage stop.

probably 150 people in the district, scattered through the valley and various mining camps."

On May 22 the expedition left for "home," via Silver Peak, and a concluding note is found in the *Territorial Enterprise* of June 10, in a "Fort Churchill Dispatch":

> Five of the Governor's exploring party —— including Messrs. Stretch, White, Butterfield, young Blasdel and Lewis, arrived here this evening, six days from Pahranagat, distance 306 miles. All well.

As with so many others they found neither gold or silver in or around Death Valley. But their efforts were richly rewarding in making the unknown better known. And their encounter with Breyfogle and the confirmation of the '49ers "Cave Spring" are invaluable contributions to Death Valley history—as well as, by elimination, that they did not find any massed Savage-Pinney bodies.

☆   ☆   ☆

Credit is given for the above to the California Division of Mines for the Appendix E material, and to the University of Nevada at Reno for the *Territorial Enterprise* articles, detailed below:

Article	Dated			Issue of	
#2	Mar	26	Montgomery	April	8
3	Mar	29	Silver Peak	April	13
4	Mar	30	Silver Peak	April	14
5	Apr	1	Silver Peak	April	15
6	Apr	8	Alida Valley Springs	April	17
7	Apr	14	Bonner's Spring	May	31
8	May	21	Silver Canyon, Pahranagat	June	6
9	June	4	Indian Springs	June	10
10	Apr	21	Furnace Creek	June	22
11	Apr	27	Furnace Creek	June	23
12	Apr	28	Furnace Creek	June	24
13	May	7	Furnace Creek	June	26
14	May	6	Furnace Creek	June	27
15	May	16	Hatfield's Ranch, Pahranagat	June	28
16	May	22	Springer's Ranch, Pahranagat	June	29

An extensive search has revealed no known copies of article #1. Number 8 and #9, and more minor #13, appeared in the *Enterprise* out of sequence, undoubtedly due to separation and delays enroute.

As noted earlier, no mention is made of how the articles were sent back to Virginia City, or by whom although presumably by "messengers" detailed to that duty. In any event, for the most part they made remarkably good time dispatched from such remote locations.

"W B Rood 1849" inscription rock on Emigrant Wash slope near Cottonwood Canyon.

"W B R 1849" inscription rock in Jayhawker Canyon.

Chapter Eight

RETURN OF ROOD & THE REVEREND

Despite ferverent avowals by one and all that they had their fill of Death Valley, two more '49ers made notable returns. One lured by the Lost Gunsight silver, the other possibly so; each shedding new light on the murky past.

W. B. Rood ✔

In April 1869, prospecting entrepreneur George Miller left the ranch of W. W. McCoy,[55] along with Paul Van Curen, Eugene Lander and W. H. Rhodes[56]:

> . . . Rhodes was one of the survivors among the emigrants who came through Death Valley in 1849 and picked up the silver out of which they made a gunsight. Mr. Rhodes told me that two men, named Martin and Townsend, brought the ore into camp at the place now known as Summit Camp, or Emigrant Pass, between Death Valley and the head of Panamint Valley, this being the second camp after they left the wagons.
>
> This was the last camp they all made together. There they killed their cattle and dried the meat as best they could to carry it along with them. They broke up into small parties there.
>
> Mr. Rhodes told me that before they separated at this place they divided up the money they had, each taking what he wanted and dumped the rest in a blanket, about $2000 or $2500, and buried it under a greasewood bush.

That the killing of cattle and drying of meat actually occurred

---

[55] McCoy was Miller's brother-in-law, per Harold and Lucile Weight's scholarly *Death Valley '49er, Arizona Pioneer, Wm. B. Rood.* Miller's account, as *A Trip to Death Valley,* also appeared in the Historical Society of Southern California's *Quarterly,* 1919.

[56] Spelled "Rude" by Manly and Doty. Others favored "Rhoods". His own letters to Colton are signed "Wm. B. Rood." Despite the phonetic variances they are of one and the same man.

at McLean Spring in Death Valley does not preclude a second slaughtering of some remaining oxen at the summit or "snow camp" where the Jayhawkers began to scatter on routes they thought best.

As to whether the money, in gold coins, was $2000, $2500, even $5000 or $6000 as reported by others, is not of great import except to those who left it and those who later sought it. Nor is the failure of Miller's prospecting party to find either the gold or silver lode. But the routes of their searchings do add new information on the '49er trails.

Traveling up Panamint Valley into Wildrose Canyon, Miller's party proceeded to:

> . . . the summit between Death Valley and Panamint Valley. There we turned east, north of Telescope Peak. There we got too far north and could not get into Death Valley. We went back southward towards Telescope Peak [and] on the west side of the canyon that came down from the peak, on a big slide that put into the canyon going east . . . we got into Death Valley east of Telescope Peak. We then went up the valley north by Bennet [sic] Wells.

Apparently they reached the 5500' summit of the steeply climbing route near Nemo Canyon, just south of the site of Harrisburg, and decided to turn east. Why they did not, or could not continue to Towne Pass is puzzling. Especially since on the open slope of that pass there is a boulder inscribed "W. B. Rood 1849" as evidence the area was familiar to Rood. Adding to this there is a second inscription, "W B R 1849" in a small canyon branching off of Towne Pass just west of Emigrant Spring. Both have long been attributed to the exit route of the '49ers. Surely Rood would not go astray with these two clues, especially with such a recognizable landmark as Telescope Peak for guidance. Except the inscriptions may not have been there in 1849! Leaving the explanation in abeyance, the Miller party, somewhat lost and confused, may well have decided to "Start from Go" at the Jayhawker "burned wagons camp" at McLean.

But first, in working their way back towards Telescope Peak, they seem to have descended the slopes near Hanaupah Canyon, canting into Death Valley near Bennett's Well. Heading north toward Furnace Creek:

> . . . we found the tracks of the emigrant wagons and the cattle trails plain to be seen. Following over those alkali flats you could see them for hundreds of yards ahead of you. We followed on until we came to Poison Spring——some call them Salt Spring—— 15 miles west [?] of Furnace Creek. This was the place where Rhodes' party left their wagons. The Indians had burnt the wagons but the irons, logchains, skeins, staples from their ox yokes and linch pins from their wagons were there.
> Some wagons had gone on far[ther] west [?] up the valley. We followed on some eight or nine miles. The tracks did not look more than six months old. We came to a sand hill blown over the tracks since the wagons had gone along. We went around . . . and found a continuation of the tracks.

That they attributed the burning of the wagons to Indians and not the '49ers who said they had done so is minor, although strange since Rood had been a participant. It is also conjectural whether the wagon tracks were all of the '49ers or those of intervening parties, including Buel, Todd, Blasdel, Breyfogle, etc. Although Miller's "west" was more northwest, it does point to the Jayhawker camps being at more than one site—one of the main party at McLean, the other of Sheldon Young's "Independents" who had continued on to near Midway Well.

But now Miller's party was on more familiar ground as they continued:

> . . . to Grapevine Spring northeast from the summit about seven miles. We stayed here and prospected a few days and then moved up about two miles to Doves Spring.[57]

---

[57] Again a bit of directional error, possibly in faulty recollection. Descriptively they headed westerly into the Panamints. While there is a Grapevine Spring near Scotty's Castle, the casual christening of springs, unknowingly renamed by others, is common. In this case the spring became best known as Emigrant Spring, near Doves Spring in the Panamints. The latter was probably named after a Captain Wm. Dove, 12th U.S. Infantry at Camp Independence, on one of the early scoutings in the area. Another version has it named for doves that often gathered there.

Chances are that enroute, resting from the steady climb up the alluvial fan of Emigrant Wash, and viewing the scenes of 1849, Rood inscribed his name and date of that earlier time. But it did not necessarily mark the '49er route for Miller's party did not directly enter Jayhawker Canyon, locale of the second Rood inscription. Instead, they entered Emigrant Canyon some easily guesstimated seven miles to Emigrant Spring before crossing the intervening ridge to Doves Spring.

Loosely located Doves' Spring was more likely Hitchen's Spring, later renamed Jayhawker Spring, for Miller notes there were signs of Indian habitations and "There were on the rocks, images of animals resembling ancient pictures." And indeed the cluster of boulders at this small but welcomed water source are inscribed with ages old petroglyphs.

By now the boulders were also inscribed with names, including Hitchens and Weston who were with the Dr. French Party nine years before. Likely inspired by such historical graffiti, Rood may well have decided, "I was here before them, so it is only fair to show it." He wasn't falsifying, simply going on record as having been there earlier.[58]

Just as all things are possible, whatever the odds, Rood might have made his inscription in 1849. But the Jayhawkers left McLean Spring on December 30. It would have taken fast, very fast, traveling indeed to permit a just under the wire dating the next and last day of '49. At least for the first inscription on the slope. And especially for the second tucked in Jayhawker Canyon. Still it might be argued that they had lost track of time, little realizing a new year had started.

Yet, however deductively, one is mindful that the laborious carving on desert hardened boulders is hardly done by men in a hurry to survive. Or chancing precious knife blades being dulled or broken just to "leave their mark." Far more likely is that the

---

[58] McCoy, although not specifically rostered, may well have been a member of the party, or a subsequent one, since "McCoy" is also inscribed on one of the boulders.

"Rood rocks," although dated 1849, were done 20 years later when time and opportunity better permitted such recording.

Returning to the Wildrose area of the Panamints, the party joined with still another group of "Gunsight" searchers, of which a Jake Phold was a member. Almost needless to say, none succeeded in finding that elusive treasure trove. Ironically, however, they were close to, and may even have crossed over the rich discoveries of Skidoo.

Rood, Van Curen and Lander returned to San Bernardino, while Miller went to work in a smelting furnace at Cerro Gordo. Rood eventually wound up mining in the Mexican border area of Arizona and was reported drowned in the Colorado River. Post-scripting his account, Miller adds an interesting if faulty account of "How the emigrants got into Death Valley":

> They got out on the desert about Amargosa and they became dissatisfied. They thought he (Captain Hunt, the guide) was taking them too far south and some of them rebelled and would not follow him and went farther west on their own account and got lost. Those who stayed with Mr. Hunt came in all right. Others who had undertaken to follow, when they came to where the wagon tracks separated, and did not know which way to go became lost in the desert. When Mr. Hunt came in he reported the facts and they got up a party and went to the rescue and brought back all they could find.

Reverend Brier

Death Valley was to call yet another of its famed '49ers—the loquacious, controversial Rev. J. W. Brier, Sr.

His revisit in 1874, nearly a quarter of a century after the trail blazing trek, was unheralded and uncorroborated. But viewed as dogma or gospel, his account provides particularly helpful specifics on their escape route trail. In a lengthy letter to Charles Mecum, dated Grass Valley, January 17, 1876, in response to an invitation to attend the 5th Jayhawker reunion,[59] he writes:

---

[59] The first reunion was in 1872 and annually thereafter with the last in 1918.

> Your letter of invitation is before me and I am sorry that I find it impossible to be present at your dwelling on the 4th of February. Your invitation brings vividly before me the sufferings and sorrows of that fearful winter of peril in the deserts.
>
> Two years ago I was induced to go back as far as Death Valley as a guide to a company of miners. The first place that I struck our old trail was at the Indian Springs where we first reached the Sierra Nevada Mtns.[60] There is a hotel now at the spot. From there to Death Valley, as it is now called, every foot of the way looked as familiar to me as though I had been there but a day before.
>
> From Indian Springs to the 1st range of Owens Mt. is 25 miles. We crossed this desert in '50 as you all remember in a little less than two days. From the spring south of the canyon that we came down to the top of the mt. where we camped is ten miles. From the summit camp to the spring found by Deacon Richards is ten miles. That spring is now called Providence Spring on account of the number of lives saved by it. From there to the lake 11 miles south ...

His second-sight mileages are not AAA accurate, but acceptable. Particularly after crossing the Coso-Argus mountains and traveling up the flat expanse of Panamint Valley:

> From the lake to the spring in Panamint Valley where Capt. Town & Co. left me and I joined the Jayhawkers[61] is 25 miles. You all remember the Muskrat [Mesquite] Swamps, Indian springs and wickeups.
>
> You remember the very high Mt. east of this point. That Mt. is the location of the celebrated Panamint Mines that were discovered since my trip back as guide. There is now a populous mining town at this point and a good stage to it, all since I was there.[62]
>
> From the Muskeet Swamp to the head of the valley, where the Mississippi boys left us is 20 miles and 20 more to Death Valley.

---

[60] Indian Wells, now Homestead, just west of Inyokern.

[61] A slip of memory. They had joined the Jayhawkers in Death Valley at McLean Spring, where the Jayhawkers burned their wagons.

[62] Panamint City, actually "founded" at least a year before (1873). The road down Surprise Canyon connected with a stage route from Ballarat, across the Argus-Cosos via Shepherd Canyon, connecting with a stage from Darwin and on to the Sierra Nevada via Mountain Springs Canyon.

> . . . At Providence Spring I found a Jayhawk ox shoe which I
> brought home as a momento. At our old camp in Town's Pass,
> where we melted snow, I found a butcher knife. At most of these
> points I wept over the remembrance of our sufferings.
> Capt. Culverwell, one of the four white men and the negro who
> overtook us in Utah, sleeps on the summit of the Panamints near
> where the mines are located. Old Father Fish fell to rise no more
> on the Mt. side [of] Panamint Valley that is west of the valley,
> and Isham his driver was buried three or four miles south of
> Providence Springs. The Jayhawks voted me his watch and pock-
> etbook. His brother came on from Michigan in '51 and found
> me in Marysville, to him I delivered his property.

Grateful as one is for much of his information it may be nit-
picking to point out a few flaws. Culverwell was one of six, not
five, and perished near the floor of Death Valley, not on a summit.
And Isham was not Fish's [Fisch] driver. And to clarify any
curiosity whether the brother was Fish's or Isham's, it was undoubtedly the latter who was from Michigan according to his
traveling companion Louis Nusbaumer.

Helpfully, Brier also adds some newsy details about other
'49ers:

> Robinson died near the Coast Range at a spring. The old French
> Man who took the wrong path . . . and was not found, was
> discovered east of Death Valley 15 years afterward in slavery to
> the relentless Diggers and was redeemed by our surveyors of the
> boundary line of the State.[63]
>
> The lady who used to tighten the girths of your oxen is still alive
> [i.e., Mrs. Brier]. The three boys are all alive. The eldest lives in
> Oakland and doing well; the youngest, Kirke, is a teacher in Oak-
> land.
>
> I will give you the names of all the Jayhawkers that I can recollect
> ——Capt. Doty, Haines, Richards, Allen who now lives in Chico,
> John Groscup, Carter, Robinson who died, Abbot of the New
> York boys, and I think two brothers named Harrison.[64]

---

[63] Undoubtedly hearsay. At least there is no mention of such an incident in any
known survey party reports.

[64] He later recalls them as the Atchison brothers.

Although there is no indication that Brier had any mining expertise there is little reason to doubt that some prospectors did "induce" him to guide them based on his familiarity with the area. Or possibly because he had been with the Jayhawkers at the scene of the Gunsight find. But there is also the suspicion of literary motives, for his 1876 letter concludes with:

> My son has published a series of poems on our trip, which he may send to your meeting.

And in his letter of January 25, 1884, to the Jayhawkers, he tells:

> My son has just finished the history of our sufferings and it is ready for the press. I hope by next spring to publish the first edition.

That the project apparently ran into snags, with Manly beating him to the punch with his classic account in 1894, lessens little the conjecture that the 1874 return may have been a refresher course for the Brier book.

In any event, Rev. Brier did not go back into Death Valley itself. Only, as he notes, "to" it. Nor, so far as known, did he return to the area again. Instead he settles for some embellished recollections in a letter to "Deacon" Richards three years later. In it he refers to the place in Nevada ". . . when we all turned south . . .", not mentioning they did so deceived by a mirage, according to his son. But startlingly takes off on a flight of fancy:

> . . . it is now certain that we were then within 40 or 50 miles of White Mt. where there is a beautiful stream of pure water running down into the head of Death Valley. . . . Grass at that point is plenty. From there, through a gentle pass, it is about 25 miles to Owens River. So you see how we missed it.

Since they had missed any such easy, certain and paradisiacal route one wonders where he obtained that visionary information. More factually he continues with some elaborations of his 1874 return with:

> . . . the valley into which we descended on New Year's day is

> Panamint Valley . . . [where] some of the Mississippi boys, with
> little West & Tom and Joe the darkies left us and steered for a
> canyon . . . now called Darwin's and at the mouth of it is a large
> mining town called Darwin City.
> You remember that we traveled down Panamint Valley 25 miles
> to some Indian springs where the mountains were very high . . .
> right up in the top of those high Mts. stands Panamint City. There
> are great silver mines.
> You remember at the foot of the Sierra Nevada some Indian
> springs . . . at this point stands now a hotel. I rode up to the door
> and told the landlord that I held a claim on the ground for I had
> slept there 25 years ago with my family. He looked stunned and
> and could scarcely believe me. . . . God bless you all . . .

Alas, the camaraderie of his letter was not to endure. It was
shattered by one of Manly's "Vermont to California" articles in
the *Santa Clara Valley Monthly,* in which Manly tells of meeting
the Jayhawkers at Indian Wells:

> I asked if the Bennetts and Arcanes teamsters had been seen and
> they said, "Yes, they were ahead with others." Where is Brier?
> "He is behind perhaps a day or two. His wife has all the camp
> work to do as well as pack the oxen for he claims he is unwell."
> Tom Shannon said he was lazy. They did not seem to have much
> sympathy for him.

To that Brier responded with a scathing denunciation in an
1898 letter:

> Shannon . . . that blackguard . . . he's paid me in full for my little
> unselfish act of kindness. This Tom of the Jayhawkers has repaid
> me in vile slander, unmitigated falsehoods . . . [and] this Manly's
> book, so called . . . and who is Louis Manly? He was one of
> Bennett's ox drivers. I did not know him but I recalled that he
> and John Rogers passed us on the desert and that they filled
> themselves with my jerk[y].

With that Brier demanded his name be stricken from any
further connection with the Jayhawkers.

In all fairness to Manly it should be noted that there is no
record of Manly and Rogers ever meeting the Briers as indicated.

It is also farfetched to picture the two feasting on the Briers'
jerky. The plight of Manly and Rogers on their rescue trek was
not that of hunger but of thirst. Both had a supply of dried meat
from the Long Camp which was to last their trek. And in his
disclaimer of knowing Manly, Brier ignores that he had hired
Manly for $50 a month as a handyman at the Los Angeles hotel
he had bought in partnership with Rev. Granger.

The on-off relationship between Brier and the others may
have smoldered for quite some time, for a reason no one seemed
to bring into the open. That of oxen. In addition to Brier's own
they had been given "a score" by Town in Death Valley. Although
Brier says he reached Los Angeles with "just two bits in pocket,"
Brier Jr. says his father "obtained a half interest in a hotel by dis-
posing of seven choice oxen out of a score." And in a letter to
Richards, Rev. Brier says he sold Captain Doty seven oxen for
$115. Since the hotel comprised a bakery, barber shop, blacksmith
shop and a vineyard, the relative affluence among the impoverish-
ed '49ers was undoubtedly envied and rankled.

Whatever his faults and failings, much is owed to Rev. Brier
who saw his family through "the valley of death," and by those
seeking to retrace their historic way.

Chapter Nine

THE BOOMERS

In a somewhat lighter vein one would be remiss not to touch upon at least a few of the adventurers into Death Valley in the late 1860's and early 70's. There were undoubtedly many. Some in small parties, some alone. Some were just passing through. Some stayed—in unmarked graves. And some who claimed a bit of Death Valley fame may have done so only by pen. However arbitrarily, although hopefully with understanding, three have been selected to exemplify all.

Dr. Willing

Between the mushrooming mining camps of Nevada and their California counterparts, a trickling tide of boom and bust fortune seekers ebbed and flowed through and around Death Valley. Now and then a glimpse of their shadows are seen in small items in old newspapers. Such as that in the *Reese River Reveille*, April 24, 1865, of a Dr. George Willing:

> Last summer Dr. Willing, with an extensive exploring party fitted out from St. Louis, Mo., attempting to penetrate Death Valley and the surrounding region. But they were compelled to desist and returned to the Owen's River country and passed south to the Colorado and Los Angeles road and then into Arizona. The doctor gives in the *St. Louis Republican* a long and graphic account of his attempt to penetrate that singular portion of the Great Basin.

From the *Republican* article, datelined "Fort Union, New Mexico, April 4, 1865," it appears 23 men left Philadelphia in December 1863 by steamer to San Francisco. There the party had a falling out. Leaving Willing behind, the rest headed for Fort Mohave on the Colorado. But Willing joined another outfit of six men, setting out on May 24, 1864 "on a perilous tour":

> A thorough exploration was given to all that country lying south of West Walker River and east of the Sierra Nevada mountains, extending even to the great Death Valley at its extreme northern end and south. . . . The entire region of the White Mountains, the Telescope Range, the Coso and Slate ranges . . . were strictly noted and passed over . . .

Was the Gunsight the magnet that drew them into that area? Probably. But as with so many others, they failed in such a quest and apparently returned to Owens Valley, deciding to follow the original company to Arizona.

But just who was Dr. Willing? One gathers he was also very able, for from bits and pieces it is learned that he was "a physician and a good geologist and a most polished gentleman." And that he had traveled over the Santa Fé Trail in 1859 and became a candidate for the office of delegate to Congress from the "Territory of Jefferson" (Colorado), going to Washington in 1860 in a futile attempt to further that cause. It was also noted, "Dr. Willing was a friend of John C. Frémont and had accompanied him on two trips out West."

Obviously Dr. Willing was stricken with mining fever, a coincidental weakness of so many doctors of that time for adventure and the excitement of treasures that lured men of all walks of life. There is no record of just where he may have gone in Death Valley. Even his personal trail has faded away. Except for a rumor of being involved in the infamous Peralta Gold Mines. And another that he was jailed as a Confederate sympathizer during the Civil War. And on a solemn note, that he died at Santa Fé.

James Hobbs

James Hobbs is one of the more controversial truth-or-fiction figures. In 1872 "Captain" Hobbs carved his Death Valley niche with his autobiographical *Wild Life In the Far West—the Per-*

sonal Adventures of a Border Mountain Man. How much is fancy, how much is fact, is debatable. Allowing the benefit of doubt, Hobbs was adventuring in the area about 1868. Although more circumstantial than substantial, his account presents some provocative possibilities.

After selling his mules to a "Mr. Nadieu"[65] at Cerro Gordo, Hobbs became acquainted with a Dutchman named Honn:

> . . . who told me he came from Salt Lake City by way of the Death Valley country which he considered very rich in the way of minerals and proposed to me to go with him and prospect . . .

Accompanied by a third partner named Hunter, they set out in search of the Gunsight Lode. That they did so is not as surprising as Hobbs' story of the source of their guidance:

> During the year 1852 an emigrant train lost their way and with one exception all perished. The man who survived, whom we met, gave an account of a rich silver mine which was discovered by one of those who perished. The man who found this mine made a gunsight of a piece of the metal, which gave to the mine the name "Gunsight Lode." We tried to induce our informant to accompany us to this mine but he declined saying he had passed through enough in that section already and never wished to return there.

Failing in their first trek, Hobbs and Hunter soon made another, resulting in Hunter declaring, "He had seen all he wished of that country and would not return there if the whole country was a solid mass of gold." But a second attempt was made and:

> We were surprised by the appearance of two Americans who rode into our camp, one of whom had an arrow sticking in his shoulder. His name was Wilson and that of his companion was John Patterson . . . [who] in company with two others had come into the valley prospecting.

---

[65] Likely Remi Nadeau, the famous early California freighter throughout the Inyo-Panamint region.

Later in his book, in an unfortunately undated retrospective incident:

> The United States government wished to make a survey of the almost unknown country about Death Valley, and to lay out a route from Fort Independence, Inyo County, to Fort Mojave, and an expedition was ordered for that purpose. The commanding officer of this expedition, Captain Andrew McFarland, heard of my experience in that desolate region and wished to engage me as a guide. . . . We started from Fort Independence with 85 soldiers.

Informatively nothing more follows, except to note there was:

> . . . a mountain where there were some very rich diggings . . . we started for it, to which on our arrival we gave the name of "Telescope Mountain" from it being very high, with the top covered with perpetual snow.

While the National Archives contain such historical gems as the maps of the scoutings of the 12th U.S. Infantry stationed at Camp Independence, they do not reveal the roster listings of any Captain McFarland (or MacFarland). Nor do the records of the War Department. Neither does the authoritative *Historical Register and Dictionary of the United States Army* by Francis Heitman reveal an officer of that name at that time.

Yet—according to desert historian E. I. Edwards, back in 1862 two brothers, Andy and John McFarland, were involved with a stage line toll road between Walker Pass, Kernville and Visalia. And that as a result of an altercation, John killed a Rod Ellis. Was this the thin thread of a name that Hobbs endeavored to weave into whole cloth? Did Hobbs associate with an Andrew McFarland and knowingly or otherwise glamorize him with the trappings of military rank and legitimacy? Or was it a figment of a fertile imagination? *Quien sabe?*

And was Honn phonetically the Hahn lauded by Lt. Bendire in 1867 and mysteriously "lost" by Lt. Wheeler in 1871?[66]

---

[66]See pages 93, 97.

Was Wilson the person for whom the Death Valley "well," noted by Blasdel in 1866, was named?

Was Hunter the "W. L. Hunter" of early Cerro Gordo and Ubehebe days, and the "Hunter's Point" noted by Dr. George in 1860?

Did Hobbs, despite the implausible version of the emigrant train, meet one of the several '49ers involved in the Gunsight find?

Could his McFarland have been a confusion of names with Farley of the Dr. French Party of 1860 and of which Lillard, credited with naming Telescope Peak, was also a member?

The number of disquieting coincidences and conflicts lead one to suspect that at least some of Hobbs' experiences were adopted and adapted for the sake of a good story that might seem more factual written as a first-hand account rather than something he had heard. For example, early Californian Don Benito Wilson was on a punitive expedition in Bear Valley, near San Bernardino, in 1845, when struck in the shoulder by a renegade's arrow and his life saved by a companion. The coincidental names, weapon and shoulder wound is suspicious, but perhaps unjustly.

Certainly nothing is impossible, although the odds may be stretched to the breaking point at times. Armchair adventurer and imaginative writer he may well have been. One can only conjecture as to what is wheat and chaff.

Oliver Roberts

Somewhat less flamboyant, although perhaps only in scope, was that of a similar soldier of fortune—Oliver Roberts de la Fontaine, whose autobiography appeared as *The True Life Story of the Last of the Wells Fargo Shotgun Express Messengers* (also more briefly titled, *The Great Understander*) published in 1931.

Making usual allowances for recollections from the past, it does offer reliable accounts of life at the Darwin-Coso mines between 1863 and 1878, studded with almost forgotten sites and scenes—of Modoc, Lookout, Minnietta, the Shepherd Canyon

Toll Road and the Darwin-Mountain Springs stage. Less reliable is his account of a trip to serve an attachment on a mine and smelting furnace at Resting Springs, just east of Furnace Creek, during which, suffering from heat and dehydration in Death Valley, he revived amid the bones of a lost emigrant party!

Still, his stories ring truer than Hobbs'. From his descriptive factualness he obviously knew the area from the Cosos to the Amargosa from actual experience. While his contribution to Death Valley history is small, he is emblematic of its variety of early day people and purposes.

The inclusion of Willing, Hobbs and Roberts may well be questioned by many. Yet they cannot be ignored for, fact or fiction, they helped to give life to the Death Valley legends that similar and no less historical places failed to achieve.

Chapter Ten

BOOTS 'N SADDLES

To the clarion call of bugles another cast was to assume their roles in the drama of Death Valley. "Forty miles a day on beans and hay" detachments of mounted infantry or "cavalry." Some were career men, some seeking three meals a day (if they were lucky) and a bit of pay. The officers were not always the elite but disciplined in purpose and in filing reports.

Major Carleton

One of, if not the first such contingent, was under the command of Captain, and Brevet Major, James Carleton, 1st Dragoons, Fort Tejon. In 1860 he was ordered to the Mojave River due to Indian depredations in that section. From his Camp Cady, between Barstow and Baker,[67] punitive parties ranged the surrounding region. One of the most notable, so far as Death Valley, was that under 2nd Lt. B. F. Davis.

In his June 21, 1860 report Davis tells of going northward, reaching Saratoga Springs. From here they headed to a "Snow Mountain to the west, apparently 20 or 25 miles distant." Penetrating the Panamints, Davis and a small detachment descriptively ascended Telescope Peak:

> I estimate the mountain 7,000[68] feet above the valley. The snow still lies in small patches on its summit. There is also some Piñon timber on its top but it is neither so well watered nor timbered as one would expect.

---

[67] As throughout this section, indeed much of this book, many place names not of the time are obviously used for reader convenience. Much in the same manner, modern names for springs, etc. are shown parenthetically.

[68] Actually it is a few feet over 11,000'. (11,049')

> There was no fresh Indian sign in the vicinity; a few old Indian huts in the valley and rancheros in the mountains show that they live here at certain seasons. Mr. Brooks says they are not Pah Utes; he calls them Ponomints [sic] and says they live in the valley from this point down.

Since Pah Utes were their objective the party returned to a camp with:

> . . . a large patch of grass, three or four hundred acres in extent, in which the water is found anywhere in great abundance by digging two or three feet. They are on the western side of the valley about 45 miles from Saratoga Springs.

Indicatively, in distance and direction, this campsite may have been Bennett's Well which is on the west side. In later years one of the soldiers said they reached Furnace Creek. But the latter is known for its free flowing Travertine Springs, where there would be no need to dig for water. At first blush the acreage for Bennett's Well might seem excessive but the scattering of grass and brush extends over a large area. And its high water table, at least at times, is evidenced by the erection of a windmill in later years.

Be it six of one, half a dozen of the other, there is little question that Lt. Davis of Major Carleton's Dragoons deserves a niche of recognition.[69]

Lt. Bendire

With the cessation of the Civil War, the army was to resume its interest in the Death Valley region. It had been criss-crossed countless times since 1849-'50, but for the most part by itinerant miners and adventurers wandering over unmarked trails and leaving none in passing. Invariably distances had been guesstimated, sites and springs promiscuously named and renamed, and terrain descriptions varied according to individual views and objectives. Too, many did not or could not write of their experiences.

---

[69] For a complete account of *Carleton's Pah-Ute Campaign*, Dennis Casebier's book of that name, a 1972 publication of his *Tales of the Mojave Road* series, is highly recommended for historians and armchair adventurers.

Now the Corps of Engineers, which had absorbed the Topographical Corps, resumed activities to map and record the relatively unknown West. These men, certainly the officers, could not only write but were obliged to make detailed reports with substantiating maps.

Several years before the more extensive Wheeler explorations, 1st Lt. Charles Bendire[70] left Camp Independence, Inyo County, on April 6, 1867, with 25 men of Co. D, 1st U.S. Cavalry and four civilian guides and packers.

Proceeding to Lone Pine, the party continued to the Coso mines along the old wagon road through Centennial Flat to Granite Springs. From here they struck southeasterly through Etcharren Valley to "Neil Spring" (possibly LaMotte or Margaret Ann Spring) in the Argus Range near Shepherd Canyon. Wending their way down the slopes into Panamint Valley they turned south, around the Slate Range, into the lower arm of Panamint Valley.

At this point in his journal (April 12, 1867) Bendire names a "Mr. Hahn" as one of his guides. Chances are this was the same Hahn who was to later mysteriously disappear while accompanying Lt. Lyle and Lt. Wheeler in 1871.

Camping near "Windy Gap," 1st Sgt. Neale and nine men were detached to go through "Emigrant Canyon" and rejoin the main group at Salt Springs near the Amargosa.

(However interruptively it may be well to comment upon the relative familiarity of names and places by this time. Much of this may be due to other scoutings, evidenced by the maps of Co. B and D, 12th U.S. Infantry, also stationed at Camp Independence. While those that have surfaced are from 1873 to 1876, there may well have been earlier be it unmapped scoutings throughout the area.)

---

[70] Also spelled "Bendere" at times. Bendire Canyon, just north of Shepherd Canyon in the Argus Range was named for him.

Bendire's "Emigrant Canyon" was not the presently named one farther north. More likely it was Redlands Canyon[71] for:

> ....following up the canyon, Sgt. Neale camped at Anvil Springs [where] the Sgt. found an anvil, wagon tire and considerable old iron.

This seems to have been Anvil Spring, in Butte Valley, for which the Bennett-Alvord prospecting party is credited with naming.[72]

While Neale's detachment continued eastward, probably via Warm Springs Canyon, a wide beckoning way, Lt. Bendire was paralleling his route a little to the south via Wingate Wash and/or Long Valley and Leach Lake.[73] In any event, at the south end of Death Valley, on April 17:

> . . . after searching for a trail for some time I found some old wagon tracks which I followed in an easterly direction and arrived at Salt Springs.[74] [Here] I found the remains of several adobe houses which had been built by miners and also an old quartz mill.

Joined by Neale, the expedition headed north. With the usual obscurities that frustrate the retracing of old trails, one can only piece together Bendire's route with reasonable approximations—along the Amargosa, past Tecopa and Shoshone to near Lathrop Wells. Skirting the Spector Range they camped at "Elliot (Cane) Springs." After a "N 17 W" march of 42 miles "over an extensive desert," they reached what they named "Oak Spring . . . about the same latitude as Big Pine." Corroborating directions, distances and latitude fit with a route through the AEC's Yucca Flat to Oak Springs in the Belted Range—a route coincidentally approximating that of the Death Valleyites of 1849.

---

[71] Coincidentally and appropriately, the route of Manly, Rogers and the Long Camp Party.

[72] See pages 35, 39.

[73] Later a borax route. Lt. Wheeler maps Bendire's trail into Wingate Wash with the continuance as Long Valley. Perhaps Bendire had swung into the Leach Lake area through a pass near Lost Lake.

[74] Near the junction of Cal-127 and the gravel road near Saratoga Springs.

After camping at the base of Timpiute (Tem Piute) Peak on April 28th they veered east to Logan Springs in the Pahranagat district, securing directions to Silver Peak. Their return trek was via Quinn's Canyon, Antelope (Railroad) Valley, Shenandoah (Reveille) Valley and Monitor Valley (Cactus Flat), arriving at Black Butte, east of Tonopah, on May 10.

All of these geographical details may bog the reader down a bit, but they do give well deserved credit to this intrepid party with an awesome accomplishment in a harsh country, and with a long haul still ahead.

Crossing Ralston Valley south of the old mining town of Manhattan, they continued across Smoky Valley and the Red Mountains (Monte Cristo Range), "leaving Silver Peak 20 miles to the east," resting at the Military Station in Fish Lake Valley.[75] Departing on the 19th they continued to Deep Spring and the Owens River, arriving at Camp Independence on May 22nd, after a month and a half in the saddle.

Lt. Bendire's report concludes with a summarization of which the following are interesting fragments:

> More than four acres suitable for agriculture I have not seen west of Pahranagat Valley in any place. The Amargosa is an insignificant brook, at least it was nothing more when I saw it, and does not deserve the name of a river. During the summer months I suppose it dries up altogether . . .

> More than half the way I made my own trail and saw no evidence of the country having been previously traveled by horse or man. Four miles south of Elliot Spring I crossed what I took to be Gov. Blasdel's trail . . .

> I expected that a good many of the animals would give out on the way but in this I was agreeably disappointed and I find that the California horses furnished to the company are well adapted for traveling in this country. Of the 16 animals with which I started I lost one . . .

> Most of the men returned bare-footed to the Post. New govern-

---

[75] Probably the small garrison stationed near Palmetto, decommissioned in 1872.

ment boots in many instances lasting no longer than one week . . . The men behaved well and the four civilians accompanying the expedition as guides and packers obeyed every order promptly and cheerfully. To Mr. Hahn more especially I am much indebted for it is entirely owing to his indomitable energy and shrewdness in finding water that I was enabled to bring the animals back in as good condition as was the case. As a mountaineer Mr. Hahn has few equals and no superiors.

Lt. Bendire's contact with Death Valley was, of course, limited to the south end. And, musingly, his report was evidently never published. Yet assuredly it is one of the earliest authoritative accounts of travel through the region. It is not recorded whether he was ever commended for an assignment "Well done!" And his account, given more to matter of factness than dramatic embellishments may have occasioned it being glossed over by others. But in its quiet unassuming way, the Bendire scoutings well deserve honorable mention in the annals of the Death Valley country.

Lt. Wheeler

Far better known are the extensively detailed and mapped activities of 1st Lt. George Wheeler, in charge of the Corps of Engineer explorations in Nevada and California to:

> . . . obtain correct topographical knowledge of the country . . . ascertain as far as practicable everything relating to the physical features of the country . . . the numbers, habits and dispositions of the Indians . . . the selection of such sites as may be of use for future military operations . . . and the facilities offered for making rail or common roads.

So far as Death Valley history, Wheeler's chronicles begin with an encampment, July 23, 1871, at Naquinta Spring near the old mining camp of Tem Piute, Nevada.[76]

A separate segment of his party had assembled at Belmont, to

---

[76] Wheeler also made an earlier reconnaissance of Nevada, June-November 1869, from Ruby Valley south through Meadow Valley. The return from Indian Springs to the Pahranagat was via Quartz and Summit Springs in the AEC area, along an old route of early prospectors and settlers for many years.

the northwest, under 2nd Lt. D. A. Lyle who, in the inimitable manner of the military, had just been transferred to the hot heartland of Nevada from Alaskan duty. Leaving July 3 this detachment crossed Westgard Pass, arriving at Camp Independence on the 18th. Three days later they returned cross-country via Waucoba Spring in the upper end of Saline Valley, Eureka Valley and Sand Springs in northern Death Valley, an empty rugged land even today. Along the way their guide, "C. F. Hahn," seemingly the same Hahn so highly commended by Bendire four years earlier, mysteriously disappeared. Ostensibly he had set out to check the water supply at Grapevine Springs, near Scotty's Castle, and was never heard from again. A *Delta* newspaper item reports his field glasses were found near Sand Springs and that the bones of a Mr. Egan, also a Wheeler guide, were found along the "Rose Spring Trail across the valley."

John Spears, in his 1892 *Illustrated Sketches of Death Valley*, tells a tale that the guide, balking in his assignment, was compelled to do so by two soldiers at bayonet point. And that while the soldiers were found, the guide had "become insane, wandering away and was never found."

Fanciful? Perhaps. Spears, a newspaperman, was given to some reportorial embellishments of his 1891 trip to Death Valley. But basically his book, appearing two years before Manly's, is a prime source of early information, including some of the first photos of Death Valley.[77]

Be it as it may, after Lyle rejoined Wheeler the combined company proceeded to Camp Independence via the Westgard Pass route. Here a detachment under a Lt. Lockwood wended its way to the Randsburg area, Saratoga Springs and on east, while Lts. Lyle and Wheeler stopped just south of Lone Pine. "At this point," Lyle reported to Wheeler, "you left us and passing Cerro Gordo were going to run a reconnaissance line to the north of the mine and then join me in the Telescope Range."

---

[77] Published by Rand McNally & Co., 1892, and reprinted by Sagebrush Press in 1977. Also excerpted in the *California Illustrated* Magazine, February 1893.

At that rendezvous there is a fateful reminder of the *Delta* reference to Egan, as Lyle reports:

> . . . dispatching Mr. Egan, the guide, who so kindly volunteered to lead us to this point, with two men, to go to Cottonwood Canyon some distance up the range, there to meet and conduct you [i.e., Wheeler] to my camp.

Later that same day, following Egan's departure, Wheeler rejoined Lyle near Wildrose and assumed command of the party. But Egan, like Hahn earlier, and under strangely similar circumstances, also mysteriously disappears, never to be seen again!

Frustratingly, the Wheeler-Lyle trails are difficult to retrace accurately at times, despite Wheeler's detailed mappings. Generally one group under Wheeler proceeded from Cerro Gordo to Cottonwood Canyon. And a second, under Lyle, roughly paralleled him to the south via Darwin to Wildrose. As part of their practice to subdivide into smaller parties to fan out in covering as much area as possible, one subgroup left the Darwin area more directly west, crossing the Argus (mapped as the "Tortoise Range") to Lookout Hill.

Lyle touches upon Egan's fate:

> Several days after, when the side party [Wheeler's] from Cottonwood joined us at Ash Meadows, I learned that Mr. Egan had never joined them and was supposed to have lost himself in Death Valley.

One wonders about Egan, as guide, "losing himself." And whether Egan and Hahn perished together or in separate incidents. Was it a code of silence or simply that the others didn't know much more than we do today?

In any event, from the Telescope area, they descended the slopes approximating Blackwater Canyon, crossed Death Valley and set up a base camp at Furnace Creek. From this they continued to the Amargosa via a canyon north of Pyramid Peak, but seemingly south of Echo Canyon, possibly the cut-off used by

Col. Washington's survey party of 1854.[78] Eventually all continued eastward over the Old Spanish Trail via Ash Meadows, Pahrump, Stump Spring and Mountain Spring to Tucson and the Colorado River.

Tucked away in Wheeler's account are some items of particular interest on the 1849ers. For example, his mapping of Town's Pass as *south* of Pinto Peak, cluing the '49er escape route south of the presently designated pass. There is also still another scrambled account of the "Route Taken by Emigrants Perishing in and near Death Valley," appearing in his Preliminary Report of 1869:

> These parties, consisting of as many as forty wagons and one hundred and fifty souls, having crossed the plains and reached Salt Lake, passed to the south and west through some of the Mormon settlements until the vicinity of Meadow Valley was reached. From this point a Mormon named Bennett was to guide them through to California.[79]
>
> Passing to the westward of Meadow Valley, a spring in the foothills of the continuation of the Schell Creek Range, now known as Bennett's Spring was reached. From this point . . . bearing to the north and west, they wandered until the sink of Sierra Creek [i.e., near Hot Creek in the Pahroc Range] was reached.
>
> At this place Bennett deserted them, leaving behind him no information, and the parties themselves at a poor and sterile camp, while he returned to some of the settlements where he is still living.
>
> Starting out from Sierra Creek and traveling nearly due west, they wandered over the mountain desert, traveling for the most part well down in the valleys, not realizing that more frequently water must be sought up among the foothills. Suffering soon arose and the large party broke up into several small ones, wandering here and there until the men, exhausted by thirst and fatigue, and the animals for the want of sustenance and water, the great Death Valley of Southwestern Nevada made for them a grave.

---

[78]See page 31.

[79]Mormon Jefferson Hunt was the guide, not Bennett, who was one of the '49ers. Wheeler is unwittingly mixing the account with that of a Mormon expedition with James Martineau in 1858, guided by Bennett who had turned Mormon by then, and for whom Bennett Spring(s) in the Highland Range near Panaca was named by that party.

Chance parties of prospectors and explorers have found the bones of the men and animals and remnants of the wagons at desert points as far to the southwest as Death Valley proper. Iron tires taken from the old wagons were found by us at the mines in Meadow Valley and at Las Vegas Ranch.[80]

An old Indian once told our interpreter that he had followed after the parties, wishing to give information in regard to the springs, but that they were much afraid of him and would not let him come within hailing distance, preferring to perish in the rough, wild desert rather than trust themselves in the hands of treacherous Indians.[81] Their loss is a sad example of the misfortunes of mountain travel where, with no one to lead, and no prior knowledge of the country, parties may meet with the most intense hardship and suffering if not, in the above case, the most wretched of deaths.

However flawed the version, it does point up that even as late as 1869-71, and by so eminent a person as Wheeler, the story of the '49ers was still clouded by a haze of fancy accepted as fact, of gossip repeated as gospel, of threads of truth fabricated into whole cloth.

Lt. Birnie

The closing chapter of the colorful "boots 'n saddles" men began on July 23, 1875, when Lt. Roger Birnie of the 13th Infantry concluded the Wheeler explorations with a mid-summer trek into Death Valley.

Lt. Birnie, with a party of seven others, left camp near Los Angeles, proceeding northward to the vicinity of Harper Dry Lake and Pilot Knob, then westward, south of Searles Lake, to the Sierra. While this leg of their journey is not directly pertinent to Death Valley it does contain interesting observations of the area at that time.

---

[80] In an 1894 letter, Manly writes that Indians found tire irons at Sand Springs, Nevada, and sold them in Pioche near Meadow Valley. And Thompson & West's *History of Nevada, 1881*, reports Indians farming there with "picks and spades" made from abandoned emigrant wagons.

[81] This is in contrast to the '49er account of capturing Indians who did show them springs, such as in the Sand Springs area near Tem Piute.

From Granite Springs, near the base of Pilot Knob:

> . . . the party moved westerly by way of Surveyors Well and Willow Tree Spring to Panamint Station[82] over an old and little used wagon road, passing by the El Paso silver mines that have not been worked for several years.

From Olancha Peak they swung eastward to Darwin and Coso—"an old but now abandoned gold-quartz mining town, except by a few Mexicans."

> From Coso, following a wagon road, we crossed the Argus range into Shepherd Canyon and thence directly across Panamint Valley to Canyon Station in Panamint or Surprise Canyon. . . . We remained about a month [until August 28th], occupied in measuring a check line base in Panamint Valley, an ascent of Telescope Peak, a trip to Lookout and Rose Spring mining districts and another to Panamint [City].

Apparently, following a by now well established Shepherd Canyon route between Coso and the Panamints, Lt. Birnie's party camped at Chris Wicht's old oasis-like camp just inside Surprise Canyon, where ample water, shade and forage made it an ideal base for the Panamint explorations. From Panamint City, then in its heyday, they crossed the steep summit trail into Johnson Canyon, passing "Hungry Bill's Ranch" which supplied Panamint City with fresh produce.

> The first portion of the descent to Death Valley was very steep. In the canyon through which we passed grass and a short running stream were found, also a small cultivated piece of ground where vegetables were raised by irrigation.
> Entering Death Valley we turned northward and camped two days at Bennett's Wells nearly on the edge of the great alkaline deposit of the valley; but permanent and very good water, only a little alkaline was found in the wells——three or four holes scarcely more than six feet deep——while coarse green bunched grass furnished pasture for the animals and mesquite trees grew

---

[82] A station of the Cerro Gordo Freighting Company, mapped by Co. D. Camp Independence, as near Indian Wells at present day Freeman Junction to Walker Pass.

sparsely around . . . the flat portion of the valley about five miles wide . . .

Were they really at Bennett's Well—or one of the other wells/springs along that section? He does not note any signs of the '49er "Long Camp," although they could have disappeared in the span of 25 years. But he does report passing "two fresh water springs, both somewhat medicinal" as they moved northerly:

> . . . along the western border and crossed to the northeast over the old emigrant road to Furnace Creek. . . . We did not suffer as much from the heat as we had anticipated although the thermometer was noted at one time at 145°. . .

In the meantime, part of the contingent, which had separated in Surprise Canyon, had gone south to "Leach's Point and Owl Springs to Saratoga Springs . . . thence by Ash Meadows to our camp at Furnace Creek," which they "reached September 8, having been [enroute] about 13 days."

From Furnace Creek the united party crossed the Funeral Mountains "by a pass heretofore unexplored" to Oasis Valley (near Beatty), swerving back into Death Valley via Boundary Canyon to "Salt Wells":

> We found the water at Salt Wells unfit for use but in crossing the valley and at a short distance from our camp we found several holes with a small supply of good water . . . the valley here is about 12 miles wide.

Considering their subsequent exit via Cottonwood Canyon, Lt. Birnie's troop either reached McLean Spring or "Salt Well" just east of it. But again, as at Bennett's Well, there is no reference to the finding of any '49er camp signs. Whether they had disappeared with time, cloudbursts, shifting sands, or were simply chalked off to now common mining activities, remains unknown.

Arriving at Camp Independence after two and a half months on the trail, Lt. Birnie's party can be credited with an appreciation of Death Valley in summer that few of his predecessors knew and were doubtless happy to avoid. And whatever its failings of historical import, their achievements were above and beyond the call of routine duty.

Beaver Dam wilderness area, straddling
the Nevada-Utah border . . .

. . . and Bigler's inscription near the
base of one of the cliffs.

Along the route up
the opposite side a "49"
carved in the sidewall.

Chapter Eleven

LETTERS OF FIRE, TABLETS OF STONE

Perhaps as a welcome break from the necessarily detailed accounts are a collection of inscriptions that mark the passage of the 1849ers in their epic trek across central Nevada and Death Valley. Few have seen any, fewer still all. One has never been found and two, unrelated, but along the trail, are inexplainable. The authenticity of the inscriptions has been questioned, attributing some to practical jokers. Yet they are in little known areas, bleak and remote back then and much the same today, where any future viewers would be rare, especially those aware of their significance.

Bigler

The first of these is that of Henry W. Bigler, on a footwall of "Mt. Misery" which the '49ers first found impassible. Although not a Death Valleyite, '49er Bigler was among the "horse and mule packers" who found a route down the steep cliffs. His journal entry for November 3, 1849 reads:

> Laid by until nearly noon for our animals to rest and eat grass.
> I cut the three first letters of my name on a rock and the date.

Although the date has been partially obliterated his initials— H W B and "18—" can still be found, be it with difficulty and preferrably with good guidance.[83] More than merely an inscrip-

---

[83] Fatefully, it was on January 24, 1848 that Bigler, one of the Mormons helping to build Sutter's sawmill at Coloma, recorded, "This day some kind of mettle was found in the tail of the race that looks like goald, first discovered by James Martial, the Boss of the Mill." Footnoting this history-touched man, after reaching Los Angeles Bigler and others of his "horse and mule packers" continued to Hawaii (then called the Sandwich Isles), arriving December 12, 1850, as Mormon missionaries.

tion it keys the descent of the Death Valley group with their wagons a week later.

"Osborn" ✔

From the meadowland at the bottom of Mt. Misery, a half mile or so from the Bigler inscription, the '49ers found a route up the opposite side. On a sandstone cliff wall are an array of carvings, most of latter-day pioneers, including Hamblin, Pulsipher and other early settlers. Among them is the name "Osborn" and an adjoining "49." No Osborn has been found in any '49er listing. However it is doubtful that the date goes with that name. Rather, to indecipherably weathered initials adjoining. Supported by the journal descriptions of '49er Sheldon Young and Asa Haines, it points the way of the "shortcutters" as they continued westward and into history.

Erkson ✔

Alas no one has yet found the inscription by Alexander Erkson who did not descend Mt. Misery, but instead turned back to rejoin the wagons that remained with Captain Hunt:

> On my way back from Mt. Misery I climbed up on a big rock and inscribed the date——Nov. 10, 1849.

It may well have eroded away in over a hundred years since, yet somewhere on the rugged slopes, close to Pine Park Canyon that feeds into Beaver Dam-Meadow Valley Wash, it may still be found by some intrepid searcher, just as others, also seemingly as lost, have been.

Nye Canyon ✔

In the area long closed off by the AEC there is an old historic route through Nye Canyon, actually more of a wide, sandy wash for the most part. Midway, just south of a series of notable cavities (observed by Manly, as ". . . niches or cavities as large as a barrel or larger") a rocky projection is inscribed, "Triple Tanks ¼ mile." This points the way to some water-catching rock basins at the end of a small ravine, with the inscription attributed to an early railroad survey team.

More importantly, adjoining it and an array of petroglyphs, is the date "1849." It unmistakably marks the route and camp of the Bennetts, Arcans and fellow traveler Louis Nusbaumer who details and dates it as December 7 and 8, 1849.

Marble Canyon ✔

Just above the junction of Marble Canyon and Cottonwood Canyon before they empty into Death Valley is another 1849 inscription. It marks the route of '49er Sheldon Young's small party of "Independents" who had camped near Midway Well, having passed nearby McLean Spring as having insufficient water and forage with the Jayhawkers already encamped there.

Heading westerly from Midway Well on December 30, Young's group entered the canyon opening and camped that night just within the Marble Canyon branching.

That the inscription, in a relatively accessible area, is so little known is due to being pecked out in a series of dots, rather than carved. Surrounded by an array of similarly pecked petroglyphs one can easily stand only a few feet away and not see the "1849" —until suddenly it leaps out to the eye of the beholder, especially when guided by those who *know* it is there.

Rood ✔

There are, of course, two other "49er rocks"—one on the slopes of Emigrant Wash, the other in the side-spur Jayhawker Canyon, just south of Towne Pass. As covered in pages 75-79 they are attributed to Jayhawker William Rood. Whether he did so in 1849, or 20 years later when he returned with a party of prospectors, matters little. They do point out the general exodus of the '49ers from Death Valley.

"1848" ✔

Of the two mystery inscriptions, one is just off of Nye Canyon, not far from Triple Tanks. Indeed it was in searching for a

"Triple Tanks" view of desolate Nye Canyon country in AEC test site . . . and 1849 inscription (below).

1848 inscription, Nye Canyon, AEC area, Nevada.

"1849", Marble Canyon, Death Valley. Pecked out, rather than carved, it is almost lost amid surrounding petroglyphs.

rumored "W L Manly" inscription that an "1848" was found in a low, concaved sandstone cliff.

Was 1848 an error? A joke by later perpetrators? Possibly. Yet rumors of other "lost wagon trains" abound. One, unverifiable, that of a wagon train that left Salt Lake City over the northern route—but in nearing the infamous Carson Sink parted ways. And that one section, under a Mr. Gann, headed south along the great sandy valleys past the future site of Tonopah and into the Nye Canyon country. According to some old settlers of the area, the remains of one of the wagons was found at Frenchman Flat.

Could it be that the '49ers were not the first to near the Amargosa not far from Death Valley? Could this be why stories of an entire wagon train perishing persist?

Byor

Possibly even more intriguing, in part because of a startling touch, is the inscription stone found at Cane Spring—the "Indian farm" reached by Manly and Rogers, which saved the Bennetts, Arcans and Nusbaumer's small contingent.

Inscribed "F. O. Byor 1847", and embellished with a skull and crossbones, it was found close to a spring that has been flowing as long as man has known. As time went on a small rock-house was built at the spring. And the inscription rock was found and placed as a center-piece in the fireplace wall. When the abode was abandoned and began to crumble, the rock was salvaged and placed in the Mackay School of Mines in Nevada.

The inscription is too finely carved to have been done casually, especially by men in a hurry. While a legendary symbol of piracy, the skull and crossbones were also oft a reverent sign of death. Combined with the permanency of the lettering, could it have been a headstone?

But who was in that God forsaken area two years before the '49ers?

Punitive expeditions had ranged out from the small pueblo of

1847 rock, Cane Springs, AEC area, Nevada.

Los Angeles in its early years, seeking to curb marauding Indians. But all possible army listings and rosters were checked to no avail. Yet they might have been civilians who often joined the military ventures, or were on their own. All that can be safely ventured is there were at least two persons—the carver and Byor, if headstone it was indeed.

But just who F. O. Byor was there is not a clue. Not even after many years of research by many who have sought a solution to the puzzle.

CHAPTER TWELVE

BACK TO MANLY—MOORE'S FLAT

THERE IS, UNDERSTANDABLY, an almost Pavlovian association of William Manly with Death Valley. Deservedly so, for it is his classic account that captures the trials and tribulations of its historic '49ers as no other. But it seems less than fair to dismiss him from mind and record once he reached Los Angeles. After all, a very sizeable portion of his book is devoted to the results of the endeavor that brought him into Death Valley. To join the gold rush.

True, in this book on Death Valley it may be stretching things —and miles—to bring in The Mother Lode. But hopefully it will be interesting to know of the relatively little acknowledged sequel of the fate of the hero of Death Valley. Especially its link with the widely known fame of the gold rush country.

Many have read Manly's book, but some have glossed over its less dramatic portions near the ending. Fewer still have given much thought to its importance. And rare indeed are those who have followed that trail.

But northeast of Nevada City-Grass Valley, in a mountainous wilderness cut deeply by the north, middle and south forks of the Yuba River, lie the sites of mining camps known only to time. And their pine-needled pathways were as familiar to Manly as Death Valley.

At first, in 1850, Manly tried mining from the Merced River and the Mariposa mines to Coloma and Georgetown with his '49er trek companion Asahel Bennett. In a small but interesting footnote to their Death Valley saga, at Georgetown their "Long Camp" dog was lost and seen no more. Here, too, Manly sold his

Alas, they do not mention Manly!

The old cemetery at Moore's Flat.

Part of "Long Tom" remains as a relic of Moore's Flat mining days.

gun and the one-eyed mule that was so instrumental in the Death Valley rescue, for 12 ounces of gold.

With less than the best of good fortune and a yearning to go "home," Manly took a ship in late November, apparently having had his fill of overland travel, to return to Wisconsin. But in 1851 he was back in California. This time to try his luck in the northern "mines" of the Yuba River area, including Goodyears Bar and Downieville. Along the Middle Fork of the Yuba he and two partners were rewarded with 40 ounces of gold—today worth about $15,000—in one afternoon!

Near "Bloody Run Ridge," deciding it was easier to get gold from the miners pockets than the ground, Manly set up a small supply store at Moore's Flat. The towering trees, steep mountains and wild rivers were undoubtedly a welcomed change from the desert sands and saline flats he had so long endured. Today, in this long abandoned site, hiking its verdant trails there is an overwhelming feeling of walking in Manly's footsteps as if in Death Valley. And in a great measure they are inseparable of this man who, as no other, symbolizes Death Valley history.

But, as with many wanderers, the time came to settle down. And in 1859 Manly bought a farm near San Jose. He married a Mary Jane Woods in 1862. After 40 years together, Manly died February 5, 1903, at 83, seven months after the death of his wife, and is buried in the Woods family plot at Woodbridge, near Lodi, California.

☆　☆　☆

Of his old friend, John Rogers, with whom he shared so much, including the heroic rescue of their party, there is a brief mention of waving farewell to each other from the decks of passing steamers at Benicia in 1854.

Forty years later Manly heard that Rogers was living near Merced, working as a ranch handyman after losing the forepart of both feet to mercury contamination in a gold processing mill.

And by train and buggy Manly paid Rogers a visit in 1895. At first they hardly recognized each other—"It had been 41 years since we last met"—and for two days and nights they reminisced before parting for the last time.[84]

---

[84]Frank Latta's *Death Valley '49ers*, Bear State Books, Santa Cruz, including two Manly letters to the Jayhawkers (one January 15, 1895 and the other undated) and a report of the reunion in the July 15, 1895 San Jose *Pioneer*.

FINALE

OF THE ERAS AND EVENTS that followed and intertwined—of Skidoo and Rhyolite . . . Greenwater, Bullfrog, the Echo Canyon Inyo Mines . . . Goldfield, Tonopah and Rawhide . . . the Tonopah and Tidewater Railroad . . . the borax boom . . . Death Valley Scotty, Shorty Harris and Seldom Seen Slim—all have had their days of fame and fortune.

Of these, and a host of other names and places, some immortalized, some lost in fading memories, much has already been written by those who knew them well. Because of this they are still part of the present as a bridge over which one may venture back into the yellowed pages of time and over trails obliterated by the swirling desert sands.

That which has been told in the preceding pages has been detailed not only for the historically inclined, but for those who look into the colorful mountains, beckoning canyons and shimmering salt flats, wondering about those who did so long before.

It is an attempt to weave together the tangled threads of the past into a pattern formed by the flickering lights and shadows of lonely campsites, and of the exciting lure of the rainbow's end even in the Valley of Death.

This book has brought you this far along those trails. The rest of the way is yours to explore, to savor.

THE EPILOGUE
THAT ISN'T

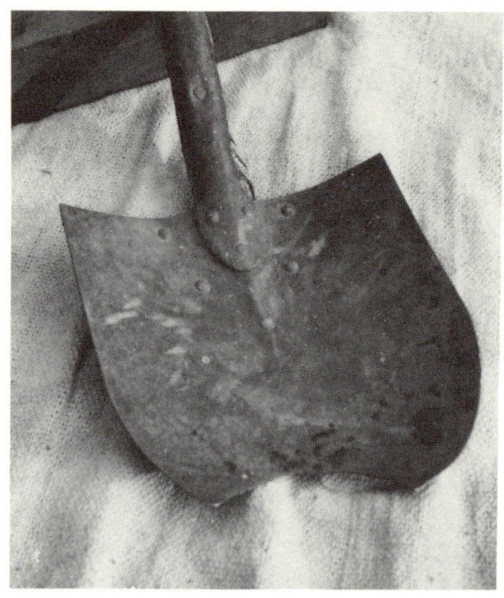

Normally an epilogue is a summarization. Or a curiosity satisfying wrap-up of what eventually happened to people, places and events. Even, occasionally, to remedy unfortunate omissions.

This is none of these.

It is simply a little story-behind-the-story of the '49ers. One that did not merit inclusion with those of historical import and scope. It is too long for a footnote, too short to stand on its own although brevity may be its virtue. It is not a great or exciting story. Yet in a quiet way it bespeaks of Death Valley's continuing delights of pursuit and discovery.

It is the story of a shovel.

ONCE UPON A TIME, back in the early days of February 1850 to be a little more precise, '49ers Manly and Rogers returned from their heroic trek to rescue the Bennett and Arcan families they had left in the "Long Camp" at Bennett's Well. In leaving, the party took a shovel to bury the body of Captain Culverwell, which they had found a few miles away. It was also used to shovel sand to cushion the descent of the oxen over a large rock falls in Redlands Canyon. Presumably, with no further foreseeable use, it was abandoned to lighten the load for the arduous days ahead.

In the early 1900's, Charles Ferge, picturesquely known as "Seldom Seen Slim," abandoned the fickle fortunes of Bullfrog and Rhyolite. Prospecting in the Panamints, he picked up a shovel in Redlands Canyon, near its unique rock falls. Perhaps more correctly, part of a shovel; the handle having been broken off a foot or so above the blade.

The wood was deeply etched by desert weathering, the blade rusty and the tip worn into a small quarter moon curvature. Perhaps "Seldom" salvaged it with thoughts of replacing the handle, or just the desert-bred instinct to keep almost anything of even remote value. Fortunately he stored it inside and under cover against further deterioration.

How and when "Seldom" became convinced it was the "Manly-Rogers shovel" no one knows. But he was surprisingly knowledgable on the subject. And cling he did to that belief, and to the shovel, for over 30 years. When he died it was bequeathed to his long time desert friend, "Pop" Lofinck, the almost legendary Outer Range Guard at the China Lake Naval Weapons Center, who in turn passed it on to another mutual friend and fellow wanderer of the area—this writer.

But was it The Shovel? The one that buried poor Culverwell, the only known '49er fatality in Death Valley? And also used to shovel the cushioning sand for the oxen? Who can say beyond all shadow of doubt?

It could have been dropped by some prospector. Even if it was The Shovel, it might have been discarded elsewhere, picked up, carried awhile and left or lost later, far from its original abandonment.

That it was old there was no doubt. But well over a hundred years old?

In the hopeful expectation that some identification of its manufacture might be made and dated, a search began for any shovel maker who might shed some light. Obviously it would be out of contention if the shovel was made after 1850. So, too, would its eligibility be lessened by a span of manufacturing before and after 1850.

With all of the odds of finding a needle in a haystack, a reply was eventually received from the O. Ames Company, makers of shovels since 1774, and whose product was literally "the shovel that built America." Checking their old records, company museum collection of shovels and staff experts, they reported: "The shovel is an old Ames back-strap shovel made between 1830 and 1850"!

True, sadly so, even though it may have been made then such shovels were in use for many years by many people in many places. And there are those who would smile knowingly, perhaps a bit too readily, at its being another tall tale. But—the finding, now over 70 years ago, of a shovel made between 1830 and 1850, in a little known canyon along the route of the '49ers out of Death Valley, brings to mind the odds against finding the Rosetta Stone.

But that was done.

The impossible can be possible.

Truth can be stranger than fiction.

RECOMMENDED READING

There are many books on Death Valley, the listing of which depends in large measure upon the personal preferences of the compiler. This is mine, for those who wish to delve more deeply into the lore and legends of early Death Valley.

Belden, L. Burr	*Goodbye, Death Valley!*
	Mines of Death Valley
	Death Valley Heroine
Clements, Dr. Thomas	*Geological Story of Death Valley*
Coolidge, Dane	*Death Valley Prospectors*
Caruthers, William	*Loafing Along Death Valley Trails*
Chalfant, W. A.	*Death Valley, The Facts*
	The Story of Inyo
Cronkhite, Daniel	*Death Valley's Victims*
Ellenbecker, John	*Jayhawkers of Death Valley*
Edwards, E. I.	*The Valley Whose Name is Death*
Glasscock, C. B.	*Gold in Them Hills*
	Here's Death Valley
Gower, Harry	*Fifty Years in Death Valley*
Greene, Linda and Latschar, John A.	*A History of Mining in Death Valley National Monument* (4 vols. NPS)
Hafen, LeRoy and Ann	*Journals of the Forty-Niners, Salt Lake to Los Angeles*
	The Old Spanish Trail
Koenig, George	*Valley of Salt, Memories of Wine*
	The Lost Death Valley '49er Journal of Louis Nusbaumer
	Beyond This Place There Be Dragons
Latta, Frank	*Death Valley '49ers*

Levy, Benjamin — *Death Valley National Monument Historical Background Study*

Long, Dr. Margaret — *Shadow of the Arrow*

Lee, Bourke — *Death Valley*
Death Valley Men

Manly, William L. — *Death Valley in '49*

Myrick, David — *Railroads of Nevada and Eastern California*

Palmer, T. S. — *Chronology of the Death Valley Region*
Place Names of the Death Valley Region in California and Nevada

Perkins, Edna — *White Heart of Mojave*

Putnam, George P. — *Death Valley and its Country*
Hickory Shirt
Death Valley Handbook

Ressler, Theo. — *Trails Divided*

Roberts, Oliver — *The Great Understander*

Spears, John R. — *Illustrated Sketches of Death Valley*

Stephens, L. Dow — *Life Sketches of a Jayhawker*

Walker, Ardis Manly — *The Manly Map*
Manly and Death Valley, Symbols of Destiny

Weight, Harold O. — *Lost Mines of Death Valley*
Twenty Mule Team Days in Death Valley
Wm. B. Rood, Death Valley '49er

Wheat, Carl I. — *Forty Niners in Death Valley*
Pioneer Visitors to Death Valley
Trailing the Forty Niners Through Death Valley

Wolff, Dr. John — *Route of the Manly Party of 1849-50 in Leaving Death Valley for the Coast*

Woodward, Arthur — *The Jayhawkers Oath and Other Sketches*
Camels and Surveyors in Death Valley

In addition there are a number of Death Valley '49er Inc., keepsakes from 1949 to present that are well worth reading and collecting.

INDEX

OTHER PUBLICATIONS
from the
DEATH VALLEY '49ers, INC.

Geological Story of Death Valley
    BY Dr. Thomas Clements

Symbols of Destiny — The Death Valley Heroism of W. L. Manly
    BY Ardis M. Walker

Death Valley Tales
    BY ten western authors

Goodbye, Death Valley
    BY L. Burr Belden

A Naturalist's Death Valley
    BY Dr. Edmund Yaeger

Camels and Surveyors in Death Valley
    BY Arthur Woodward

Fifty Years in Death Valley
    BY Harry P. Gower

Death Valley '49ers Cook Book
    EDITED BY Lydia Clements

The Lost Death Valley '49er Journal of Louis Nusbaumer
    BY George Koenig

An Unnatural History of Death Valley
    BY Paul Bailey

The text of *Death Valley Tailings* has been set in
Linotype Janson; chapter headings are Caslon. The
title page is composed of hand-set Times-Roman.
Reproduction proofs were pulled from "hot-metal"
type forms, negative and plates made thereof, and
press work performed via the lithographic process.

Of this first printing, 2,000 copies in a trade edition
have been made; an additional 275 "deluxe" copies
were bound in cloth and issued with dust jackets.